KU-732-173

God thought of sex first

John Prince

Scripture Union
47 Marylebone Lane
London W1M 6AX

© John Prince 1978

First published 1977 by ANZEA Books, Australia.
This edition published 1978 by Scripture Union,
47 Marylebone Lane, London W1M 6AX.

All Bible references are from the Good News Bible,
except where otherwise stated.

ISBN 0 85421 762 2

All Rights Reserved. No part of this publication may
be reproduced, stored in a retrieval system, or
transmitted, in any form or by any means, electronic,
mechanical, photocopying, recording or otherwise
without the prior permission of Scripture Union.

Printed by
McCorquodale (Newton) Ltd., Newton-le-Willows, Lancashire

Contents

Contents

Preface

I originally wrote this book for Australian young people but I am delighted that Scripture Union want to publish it in England. The difficulty has been to know what to change in translating it from Australian to English. Some of our everyday phrases are quite different and, of course, the young Australian male is universally a 'guy' – a word used in England alongside 'fellow', 'bloke' or 'chap' according to who you are! Incidentally in America 'guys' are of either sex!

So in the end I have changed mainly the phrases that would not be understood, would be misunderstood or would sound so funny that you would laugh at me. For the rest, I have left English readers the chance to get a little feel of the Australian language. I hope you won't object! I think you will get the message.

John Prince

Preface

1

God thought of sex first

Tony looked across the room to Jan. She was absolutely sparkling. There she went; that gorgeous tinkling laugh really sent him. It came through quite clearly over the noise that fifty-odd club members were making. As usual she was the life and soul of the group around her. Funny how she could be such good friends with all the guys and not get involved – not with him anyway, and he didn't think with any of the others either. What was it she'd said when he'd asked her out a few weeks ago? Something quite odd; oh yes, 'No thanks, Tony, it would spoil the club for me.' It was said kindly enough, but so firmly that he didn't argue and he didn't even think to ask what she meant. He still wondered.

'Hi, Tony!' Tony looked around.

'Oh! You here, Bob?' he said, trying to hide his feelings.

'Why not?' Bob paused, then following the direction Tony had been looking, he added, 'Nice, isn't she?'

'Yeah,' Tony agreed non-committally.

'She'll be good to take out tomorrow night.'

'You're not!' Tony let out more of his feelings than he intended.

'Why not?' There it was again, that cocky 'I can

have whatever I want' attitude of Bob's. It really made him mad.

'Well,' Bob nagged, 'why not, Tony?'

Tony hesitated. What he really wanted to say was, 'Because she's too good for a rat like you,' but he wasn't game. Anyway he wasn't going to let Bob see any more of what he felt. So he just said weakly, 'Well, I didn't think she went out with guys.'

'She is with me, just you wait and see!' He half shouted the last bit as he ambled across to the group where Jan was.

Tony looked at his feet. He was trying to control his feelings; with anger and some fear he had to admit there was jealousy, too. Why should Jan go out with a guy of Bob's type when she wouldn't with him? Did she know what Bob was really like, he wondered. Maybe he'd see she did.

'What's up, Tony?' Dave, one of the club leaders, was passing.

'Nothing.'

'You don't look too happy.'

'Oh, I'm all right – just thinking.'

Tony turned away and wandered outside. He could think better in the dark than in the brightly lit hall. He hardly noticed the couple in a clinch as he headed around the building. He'd never felt like this about the girls he'd taken out, or anyone else he'd wanted to take out either. That was what was getting him now. He didn't really care that Jan wouldn't come out with him. But he wasn't happy about her going with Bob – and not just because he was jealous. O.K., it wasn't his business. She didn't belong to him. But he was still worried for Jan. He knew what Bob was really like – he ought to, after all.

He and Bob had been close mates till that bust-up six months ago, so of course Bob came to him first when he struck trouble. Tony wouldn't forget in a hurry that shocking wet Monday when Bob came screaming around to his place and told him that Judy was pregnant. But how was he expected to know what Bob ought to do? He'd never even had a steady girl friend, though that wasn't for lack of trying. Nothing had clicked, that was all.

In the last six months his ideas had changed a lot, but before that he'd often wished he'd been like Bob and had a girl of his own. He wasn't so sure about the sleeping together at weekends; he and Bob had argued about that. The trouble was that Bob always won by finishing up, 'Just you wait till some bird gives you the eye and you'll soon change your mind.' 'I might, too!' Tony thought to himself.

He'd tried to warn Bob about the pregnancy bit, but he just got the brush off. How green did Tony think Bob was? Judy could get hold of the pill from a friend working in the chemist's, so there was no trouble, was there? It hadn't worked out so well, though Tony never asked him what went wrong. Perhaps they weren't as clued up on the pill and all that as Bob had said.

That Monday night came back to Tony as if it was this week. They'd sat in Bob's car, with the rain beating down so hard on the roof they just about had to shout to hear each other. That wasn't the only reason they were shouting either. Tony had ended up really annoyed and it wasn't just because Bob wanted Judy to have an abortion. That was Tony's first thought, too. It was the way Bob was only thinking about himself, what his parents would say, what Judy's parents would think of him, what the abortion would cost him. In the end Tony had told him straight.

'You're just thinking of yourself, Bob. You haven't said a thing about how it hits Judy. I don't think you really love her at all.'

'Of course I do. I got her pregnant, didn't I?'

'Oh that. That's not what I mean.'

'Well, that's love, isn't it?'

'Not the way I mean.'

'Well, what do you know about it?'

'At least I haven't got a girl pregnant, anyway.'

'Aw, shut up, Tony.'

Tony shut up. Beneath the row of words he realized something much deeper was going on. If that was Bob's attitude, he just couldn't help disliking Bob. Their friendship was falling apart in the silence. Still he had to try to help somehow.

'I reckon you need to talk to someone who knows more than me,' he said after a while.

'Like who?'

'Like Dave, up at the club,' suggested Tony, not too hopefully.

'Him?'

'Yeah, he'd know what to do.'

'What would he know about sex?'

'He ought to – running a youth club and that.'

'A *church* youth club,' spat out Bob. 'All they can talk about is being pure little boys. Don't reckon a Christian would know the first thing about sex.'

'Funny how some of 'em have kids then.'

He knew he shouldn't be saying it, even as the words came out. It wasn't the time to be funny. He tried to say he was sorry but Bob was through. He just about shoved Tony out of the car and took off before Tony could even shut the door. It slammed itself from the vicious take off, as Bob let in the clutch.

That was actually the last decent talk he'd had with Bob, if you could call it a decent talk. It had certainly started a lot. He'd seen Dave himself in the end. He'd gone to see Judy, too. That was what really fixed Bob – that Tony had persuaded Judy to tell her parents, instead of going straight ahead with what Bob was organizing. Bob had really let Tony have it for that.

Looking back, Tony realized the shake-up hadn't been all bad. Talking to Dave had opened his eyes, not so much because he had a lot of the answers. Tony had expected that. It was Dave's attitude he'd found so great. It wasn't a bit square, the way Bob had said it would be, but somehow realistic and honest. Yes, honest, that was it, for a Christian like Dave to admit he found sex a problem.

'I didn't think you'd be tempted by sex, Dave,' Tony had said.

'Why not, Tony?'

'Well, being a Christian and all that.'

'But I'm still a man, Tony.'

'Oh, sure!'

'And being a man, God made me with sex. So I feel the sex thing just as much as anyone else, whether they're Christian or not.'

'I suppose so,' Tony had replied, only half believing.

'But there is one big thing about being a Christian and following the God who made me, sex and all.'

'What's that?'

'You and I aren't the first to face the sex problem. In fact God thought of sex first and he's laid it right along the line as to how we ought to handle it. As a Christian I try and do just that.'

They'd talked a lot about it after that. Tony liked talking to Dave. Why, of course, that's what he'd do now. Dave knew all about Bob, too. He'd sort it out with Dave. Anyway it was time he went back inside.

The lights blinded him for a moment as he went in. Then he saw Dave over there with Jan's group. Bob was still hanging around there, too. Perhaps I wasn't outside so long as it seemed, Tony thought. He walked over. They were discussing next week's plans.

'Good idea,' Dave was saying. 'We'll discuss it at tomorrow night's committee meeting. You be there, Jan?'

'Sure.' Her reply pulled Tony up sharp.

'Hi, Tony, done your thinking?' Dave asked.

'Yeah,' he replied. He was thinking fast still. So Jan wasn't going out with Bob. So he didn't need to see Dave after all – or maybe he did. Not so much about Bob as about himself and how he felt about Jan.

'Yeah,' said Tony, 'I've been thinking. Say, Dave, can I talk to you for a few minutes?'

Tony was one of the lucky ones. He had someone he felt he could talk to. A lot of people haven't and that's the first reason for this book. Reading isn't as good as talking to someone you can trust who can help you sort things out, but it's better than nothing.

The second reason for this book is that many people have the wrong idea about how Christians see sex. That's partly the church's fault. Too many of the Christians who open their mouths wide about sex have little real understanding of the real problems of youth and they do a lot of harm. But it's not all their fault. Young people, like Bob, often sling off at Christians without actually knowing what Christians really think.

So this book's going to try and straighten that out. It's written for non-Christians, to let them see what the Christian idea of sex is, and it's written for Christians to help them sort out what's what in the modern world.

The best way for a Christian to do that would really be to get down to what Jesus said and what the Bible teaches. If you want to do that first, you can read chapter six before you go to chapter two. But some readers may find that a bit solid to start off with. You may find chapter six easier to take if you read the chapters in between first.

I make no apology for plugging the Christian line on sex. As Dave said, it was God who thought of sex first and so he's the one who has the answers. Our job is to find out what God's answers are. That doesn't mean that the Bible has pat answers for every twentieth century situation. Far from it. You have to work out the answers for yourself from the principles God gives you. But at least what Jesus said gives you somewhere to start and Jesus says sex is about getting married, so that's where we'll start.

2

Think big about marriage

Today's idea of marriage

Ask anyone what's behind two people getting married today and what kind of answer will you get? Top of the poll will be answers like 'They're in love' and 'They're so fond of each other'. A few may say 'They're so well matched'. How many will say 'Their families see eye to eye', or 'They want to get the legal angle straight'? Not very many! Everyone will think of a romantic personal relationship between two people. The main thing is for two people to be in love – *that's* what makes a good marriage. So goes the general line today.

It may or may not be true – it all depends on what you mean by being 'in love'. Some people mean a great emotional feeling or a hot sexual passion. Now both these things form part of many experiences of being in love, but on their own they just aren't enough. For one thing they often don't last. For another, they're only a small part of what two people need if they are to share their lives successfully. Yet lots of young people today get married on this rosy romantic picture of marriage, which comes through teenage and women's magazines, some novels and a lot of pop music. Perhaps that's one reason why the divorce rate for early marriage is quite high; many couples can't cope with what life brings along, because they haven't got a strong enough foundation.

Now the Bible doesn't rubbish the idea of having a romantic love affair. And it doesn't sweep sex under the carpet either. Far from it. You only have to look at the Boaz and Ruth love story,[1] for example. But the Bible also makes marriage something bigger than sex and bigger than a personal relationship between two people, however good that relationship may be.

The Bible just assumes that marriage has three quite different angles. It *is* a personal relationship, but it's just as much a social institution and an economic contract. People might avoid some of today's messes if they realized that all three angles are still as important as ever. It also helps to sort out the question of sex outside marriage if you get the marriage thing straight.

Marriage – a social institution

The family is the basic social institution – no one is likely to deny that. Certainly different societies mean different things by 'the family'. In a New Guinea village, or many parts of Africa, the uncles, aunts and cousins that count in the family circle would send people like us around the bend. In such a set-up a marriage has tremendous social repercussions and it will often only succeed where the families are happy about it. In our modern western culture we have come down to what sociologists call the 'nuclear family', consisting just of parents and their children. While this reduces the effect of wider family influence

[1] The Book of Ruth.

a lot, it doesn't cut it out altogether. The great heap of 'mother-in-law' jokes proves that.

It isn't just a question of interfering 'in-laws'. We all need a happy set of relationships around us if we are to find life satisfying. We find it in various ways among our circle of friends and, if we are a long way from home, that's all we may have. But the most natural place to find satisfying relationships, even when we are grown up, is the family circle. When we get married we bring someone into our family circle and we enter a new family circle ourselves. In due course the home we set up becomes a social centre for our children and so society continues on its way.

Society comes into marriage in another way, too. Marriage is never just a private agreement between two people to live together, regardless of what anyone else may say. Every society accepts the responsibility of saying who may marry who else, as far as family relationship goes. Every society accepts as properly married only those who go through the accepted routine. In primitive tribes this may be just a case of the fellow carrying the girl off, or going to her house and sleeping with her, or by some economic transaction.

Our society recognizes people as married only if they have been through a legal ceremony. It is no good two people living together and saying, 'In our eyes we are married.' They just aren't; neither in the eyes of society, nor of God. Neither their relationship nor their children are properly protected by the laws of society, because they have ignored the laws that society has made about marriage. God doesn't recognize them as married any more than they recognize the clear principles God has left us in his book, the Bible.

Marriage – an economic contract

All down the centuries and all over the world today marriage has involved an economic contract. In India today, as in Europe not so long ago, daughters count so little that you have to pay a dowry in order to get a good husband to marry your daughter. On the other hand, in tropical Africa and New Guinea daughters are the wealth of a family, as they grow all the food while their brothers sit around and talk. So parents of daughters expect a bride price payment in return for the loss of so valuable an economic asset as a daughter.

What has all that got to do with us today? Not much, I suppose, except to show you some economic aspects of marriage you may never have thought of. Society today is based on money and so the economic side of marriage still matters a lot, though the angle's different. A woman needs to have an income pro-vided during her child-rearing years. That remains true in the modern world, for no system of creches and child-care centres can satisfactorily replace mum at home to care for her children. A woman also needs to know that, if her husband dies or clears out, she's got some help while she's tied down and unable to earn a full salary. That's what the marriage law tries to give her.

Now these days both parties earn money for much of their marriage and that's fine. It gives them more scope to work out the money side of their marriage for themselves. But I must point out one snag. A girl who insists on staying too independent can give the idea that she doesn't completely trust her man – and without trust marriage hardly gets off the ground. Many men need the satisfaction of being the provider. If the girl insists on earning most of what the family needs as well as bearing the children, it doesn't leave her husband much to feel good about. Personally I feel that women's libbers, even Christian ones, can be pretty selfish in this way and it is bound to lead to trouble. The economic arrangements in any marriage have to be a true agreement – a real contract, even if it isn't written down.

Marriage – a personal partnership

From the Christian angle this is the most important of the three aspects of marriage and the standard is very high. Just listen. 'So wives must submit themselves completely to their husbands, in the same way that the church submits itself to Christ. Husbands, love your wives in the same way that Christ loves the church and gave his life for it . . . Men ought to love their wives just as they love their own bodies. A man who loves his wife loves himself . . . As the scripture says, "For this reason, a man will leave his father and mother, and unite with his wife, and the two will become one".'[1]

Paul is really saying that the best example he can find of the perfect relationship between Christ and his church is found in a Christian marriage. And the other way around, too. Christ's love for his church, even to the point of dying for it, is the kind of utterly unselfish love which a Christian couple ought to have

[1] Ephesians 5.21–31 (extracts).

for each other. Now this love expresses itself in the whole human personality. If two people are to be truly united, they will be united not only in body, but in mind or soul and in spirit. The Christian picture of marriage sees all three as of equal importance.

(a) *The union of two bodies*
The sex side of marriage is, of course, fundamental. It isn't the whole of marriage but without sex marriage doesn't exist. The New Testament is positive about that.[1] You don't find the idea that sex is unclean anywhere in it. Yet quite early in the church's life people got the idea that it was purer to live without sex than with it. That idea certainly never came from the Bible and it has no place in a true Christian view of sex. It is only the misuse of sex which the Bible sees as impure.

So the Christian can thank God for the gift of sex. Giving your body to the person you love is God's wonderful idea of expressing love between two people. It is a thing of beauty and a thing of joy, of joy which becomes even deeper when love bears fruit in the birth of a child. Anyone who has experienced the thrill of parenthood will tell you how fantastic the whole thing is. That's how God intended sex to be and his idea is just too good to be spoilt by messing about with it.

(b) *The knitting together of two people*
Marriage means sharing – at every level; sharing home, sharing money and possessions, sharing bodies and, as important as any of them, sharing ideas, thoughts and interests. Normally this sharing of

[1] *cf.* 1 Corinthians 7.1–5.

interests will come before the others during courtship days and it is best that way. It is when two people have similar ideas and interests and find they have the same approach to life that they begin to want the greater intimacy of marriage.

The sad thing is that in some marriages this delightful human fellowship seems to get lost after marriage. I've had someone say, 'We don't seem to talk much now that we are married.' How silly that is and yet it's often true; that's one way marriages land on the rocks. Marriage ought to be the ever closer knitting-together of two human beings, where each has personal interests but also a lot they share. It won't happen automatically. Like anything else, marriage has to be worked at to make it go well.

(c) *The fellowship of two spirits*
Christian marriage has an extra dimension to it which non-Christian marriage lacks. If two of you share faith in Christ, you share the deepest thing of the lot, sex included. That's why the Bible tells Christians not to be harnessed with unbelievers.[1] You may argue about whether that applies to business or sport teams or not, but it must surely apply to marriage, the most intimate human harnessing of all.

How can a Christian have a true spiritual fellowship with someone who doesn't share the same faith? It means that one partner can't share the very deepest thing in the other one's life. That makes a really satisfactory relationship impossible. There is bound to be tension on both sides. Commonly, to avoid the tension, the Christian compromises on part of the

[1] 2 Corinthians 6.14–18.

Christian life and faith gets watered down. Sometimes it just disappears altogether. That's just the opposite of what happens in a true Christian marriage, where the fellowship of faith deepens all the other sides of the marriage, too.

Incidentally, to keep the record straight for any Christian reader who is already married to a non-Christian, the Bible also makes it clear that you shouldn't break up the marriage because of that.[1] You are to live as a real Christian with that person so that they may learn about Christ from you.

Suppose I never get married

Quite a lot of people don't marry. Some just don't want to; others would like to marry very much but they don't seem to meet the right person. As a young fellow or girl you don't know how your life will work out from that angle but it is a good idea to face the possibility of staying single. It won't make you a second class citizen! In our modern world there is a lot of scope for single people of either sex and some choose to stay that way because they don't want to be restricted by family ties. They feel that the advantages of being single outweigh the advantages of being married.

The main problem is that of people who badly want to get married, but don't seem to have any prospects of doing so. Both fellows and girls naturally long for the satisfaction which a close relationship of belonging to one another gives. For most girls there is a deep fear that they may miss out on motherhood as well. So there is great pressure on people who feel

[1] 1 Corinthians 7.12–16.

these things to find someone to marry. But be careful, marrying the first person who comes along may well make you very sorry later on. To you I must say, it is far better to stay single than to rush into marriage with the wrong person.

Marriage – a life sentence

It certainly is – if you find yourself married to the wrong person! What's more this life sentence is not one which lasts till the prisoner is released on parole or by divorce. The Bible's clear that marriage is for life[1] and the Christian has to look at it that way. Children require a stable home for a secure life and only lifelong marriage provides that. Then again, commitment for life is the only way to show you trust each other enough to make marriage a success. To say, 'I'll marry you until it doesn't work out any more', means there's no real trust and that marriage has little future.

Of course, the idea of marriage for life raises the really tough question of divorce. Jesus seems to teach[2] that divorce is permissible if one partner is unfaithful, but not otherwise. Christians today are part of a secular community whose laws are different from that standard, and it is sometimes very difficult to know what stand to take. Standing for a principle may mean hurting even more someone who has already suffered a lot. So Christians find themselves divided on divorce. This isn't the place to take this difficult question apart further, though it is important to get your ideas straight before you get into the marriage

[1] Romans 7.1–3, 1 Corinthians 7.10–16.
[2] Matthew 5.32, 19.3–12.

game. If you want to read more about this I suggest you read *Divorce* by John Stott (IVP).

So marriage is for life. If you believe that, then it is a really serious thing to ask a girl to marry you or to agree to marry a guy. It's not the kind of thing you want to make a mistake about. That's the reason for the next chapter.

3

What sex is all about

So the Bible says sex is good – for marriage, but not otherwise. That really puts the Bible beyond the pale for a lot of people today. It's too square altogether. Life's changed with the pill and all that; sex is nothing to worry about any more. Or is it? Is sex outside marriage as O.K. as some people say? That's a question we'll have to answer but we're not quite ready for that yet. If you want to know how sex should be used, you've got to understand what you're using. So let's see what sex is all about.

Sex is about having children

That's obvious! These days it's possible to have sex and be pretty sure you won't have a baby, but that doesn't alter the basic fact. I'm putting this side first, not because it's the most important, but because it's the easiest. There are facts you need to know. You probably know how sex works physically, but believe it or not there are still some teenagers who don't. So in case you're one, here's a quick rundown. If you know it all, skip the next two pages. If, on the other hand, you want more information than I'm giving you here, you can get it from one of the books listed inside the back cover.

A man's sex organs consist of two glands called the

testicles and a tube called a penis. During adolescence the testicles start to produce male sex cells, called sperms, and the fluid to carry them, called semen, is also made in his body. The penis has to do a double job, acting as an outlet for urine from the bladder and as a passage for the semen during sexual intercourse.

From hearing men talk you may get the idea that, once you're adult, it's bad for you not to have sex from time to time. 'You'll be less virile if you don't,' they say. Or 'You've got to get rid of the semen some way.' Neither of those statements is true. Nature has it all under control. If there's more semen that you can hold, it comes out naturally during sleep. This is technically called a 'nocturnal emission' but people usually talk about a 'wet dream', because the emission often causes a vivid sex dream. All that's perfectly normal.

A woman's sex organs are all inside her body. The ovaries, which manufacture the human eggs (ova), are located between the hips. From each ovary a tube leads to the womb (uterus), a small pouch which is capable. of stretching enough to accommodate a baby. The womb is connected to the outside by a passage called the vagina which can also stretch greatly during the baby's birth. The opening of the vagina between a woman's legs is called the vulva.

During adolescence the changes in a girl's body prepare her for having children. The breasts develop and the menstrual cycle begins. The womb becomes lined with blood and tissue, so that a fertilized egg can grow in it if necessary. If there is no such egg then the lining breaks up and is discharged in the monthly period as a flow of blood lasting four or five days.

Then the process starts all over again for the next month.

The menstrual cycle usually starts a year or two before the ovaries become active. Then, at the time of ovulation, about two weeks before the monthly period starts, an egg is released by the ovary and moves slowly down the tube towards the womb. If it is not fertilized, it dissolves and the menstrual flow follows. If, however, the egg is fertilized by a sperm, then it embeds itself in the lining of the womb and grows there. The woman is then said to be pregnant. The cycle of menstrual periods is interrupted while the foetus grows into a baby, which, all being well, will be born nine months later.

The presence of the male sperm in the tube of the woman's body is the normal result of sexual intercourse (coitus). During lovemaking both the man's and the woman's body are suitably prepared. An inflow of blood makes the man's penis rigid so that it can penetrate into the woman's vagina, where a moist discharge is providing lubrication so that the penis won't hurt her. This final stage of lovemaking is one of intense pleasure, which gradually comes to a climax called an orgasm. Ideally both partners should reach orgasm together, but this requires practice. Often the woman finds it hard to reach orgasm at first, while the man finds it hard to hold back till she does.

The man's orgasm is accompanied by the release of semen in the vagina. Afterwards the sperms move gradually into the womb and the tubes, looking for an egg. A very large number of sperms is released in one act of intercourse and only one of these is needed to fertilize an egg if it is there. So just one act of intercourse is enough to make a girl pregnant, though it may not necessarily do so. Whether she becomes pregnant or not depends mainly on whether there is an egg present at the time the sperms have worked their way up into the tubes.

As sperms seem to be able to live inside the woman's body for some time, intercourse at any time before or around about ovulation time may lead to pregnancy. The few days around ovulation time are the most likely to lead to conception, while in the last week before the period conception is unlikely because the egg has probably dissolved already. This fact is the basis of the 'natural' methods of contraception (see chapter ten).

Sex is about loving

The mechanics of having a baby is only a small part of the story. Sex is far more than that and it affects us in a whole heap of ways. It is a basic human drive, which makes us interested in the opposite sex in the first place. The same drive makes us want a special friend of the opposite sex and gives such friendships that something special.

When we do find a friend, the sex drive operates again making us want to express our feelings physically. Holding hands, kissing, petting, heavy love-making, sexual intercourse – these are the natural steps on the road down which the sex drive wants to take us, which is all fair enough in the right place. The problem is to keep it in the right place.

Sex packs a punch

Hunger, thirst and sex are three of the most fundamental urges human beings have. They were made that way purposely, the first two to be sure we keep the life we've got going and the third to make sure we pass it on. The only thing is that in our affluent society not too many of us know what it's like to be really hungry or thirsty. Those needs just get met without our really feeling them. So it leaves sex to be coped with and there is a good reason why it takes more coping with than it used to do. In affluent societies improved nutrition and child health are making people sexually mature earlier than in the past. At the same time complex technology is making education and training last longer and longer. It's hard to get married when you've got nothing to live on and so you have to hold the sex drive in check for all that time. That's tough because the sex drive really packs a punch. You have to remember that when you're working out how to behave with the opposite sex, as we'll do in the next three chapters.

How the other half ticks

While it's the same basic sex urge that's pushing them both along, sex means two different things to the two sexes. That's why they sometimes find it a bit hard to understand each other.

Let's start with the typical girls' comment: 'Men are all the same; they're only interested in one thing from a girl.' Of course it's not true of a decent guy but there's something in it just the same. She's really saying that a man thinks a lot more quickly about physical sex than she does and she's dead right. That's the way he's made, both physically and emotionally, and she wouldn't really want it any other way.

Most often it is the man who takes the lead in sexual relations, though most men like the girl to take the lead sometimes and I think we always like to be egged on! Either way, sex can give equal pleasure to both but they work out rather differently. A man must expect to have to woo a girl subtly and gently to arouse her sexually and make her want to respond to him. By comparison, a man's sexual desires don't take much stirring up. With his sex organs outside his body, a man is naturally conscious of them. He's aware of physical sex sensations and finds them enjoyable. It's only natural that the idea of physical sex comes to his mind very easily. A girl has only to be nicely provocative and she will probably get all the active response she wants! That doesn't make him a sex fiend – just a normal man.

I think a lot of girls don't realize how easily most men are aroused, sexually. The frock that reveals more breast or thigh than usual (even if it's a lot less than he could see any day on the beach), a come-hitherish look, a slightly suggestive remark – these are three things that can easily start a man on a sex tack. And don't forget that men are just as vain as girls, only in a different way. You may *think* you never gave him any encouragement but your Romeo *knows* you did – it boosts his ego no end to think you are giving him the eye!

There's another thing, too. Sex isn't just very near the surface for a man. It's also pretty quickly over.

When he's finished making love his body is satisfied. For him sex is a short period of very great pleasure and that is the end of it. He goes on living his normal life, doing his everyday job, basically unchanged.

For a girl it's absolutely different. Her sex organs are right inside her body and she is only conscious of them through the menstrual cycle. Her sexual feelings have to be aroused for her in a way that a man's don't need to be. But those feelings run very deep indeed. If she gives herself to a man her whole life may be affected, even when a contraceptive is used. This is because psychologically a girl is geared for more than just sex.

A girl can get as much pleasure out of sex as a man does, but the act of making love is not the whole thing for her. She may never have reached a climax of pleasure herself. Yet, however much or little the act of love meant to her, it is potentially the beginning of something really big and important – motherhood. For a girl sex is the road to fulfilling her most fundamental place in life, that of bringing a new life into the world.

It is hard for a guy to realize just how deep this all goes with a girl. In a real way sex means far more to her. What's more, motherhood will make her dependent on the man in her life, emotionally as well as economically. She is being untrue to her whole feminine nature not to take sex in deadly earnest and that's something to remember for chapter five.

There are various ways in which marriage is more vital for a girl than a man. They both lose their freedom but she loses more. She doesn't just take her husband's name; she normally has to take his status in society, too. If it's very different from what her own family's was, then her whole life style has to change.

Then, too, though being a father is exciting for a man, being a mother goes a lot deeper for most girls. It goes so deep that some girls would rather have children without marriage than not have children at all.

All of this adds up to the fact that sex is really big for both sexes – though it's a different 'big' for a girl and a man. There's a lot at stake and there's a lot to understand, and a lot of people in the modern world mess it up. That's a shame, because when it's played right it's one of the finest parts of human life.

4

Getting going

So relax, you're quite normal! Of course you find the other sex interesting – mighty interesting. You've found that out? Fine, but where does that get you? Where do you go from here?

From that angle sex is much like anything else in life. You get ahead best if you've got a fair idea where you are heading and that's why we've put chapters two and three before this one. You need a good pattern of marriage and a clear idea of what sex is all about if you're going to handle friendships with the opposite sex.

Make no mistake – where you are really heading in that kind of friendship is marriage. Don't be dumb, you think, I'm only 16 or 18 or whatever and I'm not getting married for a long time yet, certainly not to that bird (guy). No fear! I'm just enjoying her (his) company. O.K., that may be how you see it, but the fact is still there; the end result of your friendship with the opposite sex is going to be, most likely, that you marry one of them.

And notice that I said *one* of them. It can't be more than one by the laws of this land, but that's not the real point. In the nature of the relationship it has to be just *one* opposite-sex friend. That's the basic difference between same sex and opposite sex friendships. If Bob and Bill are friends and Bill brings along Jack, another good mate of his, then Jack and Bob will probably become good mates, too. The same goes for Sue, Jane and Jenny. But if Bob and Jenny are close friends and Bob brings Sue along and says, 'Hi Jen, meet a very special friend of mine. She's Sue' – well, you get the point, don't you? a friendship between a guy and a girl is exclusive by nature – it cuts others right out. You try dodging that truth and you'll soon get yourself a reputation that will give you lots of time to yourself.

You can't escape the marriage bit sitting at the end of the road. You can't pretend you can be friends with the opposite sex as if two people of the opposite sex didn't get married. They do and that's that.

The fast starter

Having got that straight, it's about time to go back to the question that started the chapter. How do I get started? After all I've got to start somewhere. Do I just chat up a bird and ask her out? Or con a guy till he asks me out? Well, of course, that's one way of doing it, but there's just one snag. Which bird or guy? Will *anyone* do? Let's see how that works out.

You're a guy – sorry girls, I can't go on writing it both ways around at once, but you can put it the other way around for yourself; it applies just the same – and you chat up a girl, any girl. You've no clue what she's really like, but she'll do to learn on. You ask her out and it's fine. She's great. Of course she is; she's been dying for a guy to ask her out and now you've done just that. So she drools over you and that makes any bird great; it boosts your ego no end.

Of course you ask her out a second time. Now she really has something to talk about to her girlfriends and of course she does. She's got a boyfriend, she's going steady and she's walking on air as a result. It's a bit awkward actually, because you don't quite see it that way. In fact the second time wasn't nearly so good; you wished she didn't act as though she owned you. Still she snuggled good and close after the disco and so you couldn't really complain. Still you didn't mean to ask her out next week, so how come you did? What now? So you'll bring along a couple of others to break it down a bit.

That didn't work out too well either. Funny how the ones you asked weren't too keen on the idea. The couples wanted to be on their own and the rest had more tact than to muscle in on a couple going steady. Who said you were going steady? *You* didn't. No? Well, the idea's got around just the same. So you're nicely fixed, aren't you? O.K., she's not the girl for you; you've got nothing in common. True, but you asked her out, didn't you? So you'll just have to tell her, won't you? You don't like to? No, it will be tough! You've got an idea? What? Oh, you'll just take another girl out instead. Who? You don't know? Just any girl, so long as it's not this one? O.K., go ahead. But I've got a sort of idea that this is where we came in a page ago!

All rather silly? Maybe, but that's how it goes with a lot of kids. There's a slightly more grown-up version of the same game among those too old to be called kids. Sometimes with them it involves having sex and the works, which makes it all the harder to get disentangled from – but we'll come back to that.

There's another snag about this 'going-the-rounds' game. Some people tell you that it's good, because by going out with a lot of different people you're really getting to know the opposite sex and so you'll be really clued up to make a good final choice. It sounds good but, so far as I can see, it just doesn't work out. It seems to me that going the rounds gets you more and more confused about the opposite sex and often ends you up with someone quite unsuitable.

The slow starter

Let's just ask ourselves where our guy went astray. I've no doubt that he went in too fast, without really thinking where he was going. He'd have been much better to sit back and take a good look at the field first. Young people today are pretty lucky. With co-education fairly common, with church and community youth clubs and the rest, it's not hard to get into a group somewhere. That's the place to start – in a good mixed group of young people. There you can find out how the opposite sex ticks without getting yourself too involved. There's another thing. You get a much truer picture of someone when you see them in action with a whole lot of others of both sexes, than when you're gazing into their eyes in the moonlight.

By the way, watch out for the group that's all paired up. No doubt next month they'll be paired up quite differently; they're just going the rounds on a bigger scale and getting in the same muddle. That kind of group is no good to you. What you need is a group that really hangs together, where the guys and girls are really good friends. You feel good in a group like that and learn a lot.

If you do find someone in the group especially interesting, you at least know a bit about how they tick and can think about whether you really want to get to know them some more. But just remember to ask yourself first – do I mind getting involved? Because face it, going out with one member of the opposite sex involves you in a sort of a way, maybe only a little bit the first time, but a little bit at least. How much it involves you depends on the circumstances and your age. If you're 16 and take a schoolfriend as partner for the school disco, that amounts to just about nothing. If you're 24 and you ask a girl you don't often see out to an expensive dinner, then the chances are there's something in it. Then there's everything in between. You ought to be smart enough to work out where you fit in.

Taking a girl out, or going out with a guy, may not mean much once. But do it a second time and it begins to mean something, and after a few times you're both hooked! You're going steady. You may not think so, either of you, but the gang know the situation. More likely they have everything lined up and they'll make it happen unless you do something to stop it quickly. They're only being kind and tactful – making it easy for you. Who wouldn't help a nice romance along, after all?

What is she thinking?

There's another thing to watch, too. Remember how differently the two sexes look at sex? Well, they look at going out differently, too. The guy may well not be very serious; he just wants a girl around. Being a decent type he spells it out quite clearly. Fine! She hears his words but she doesn't really get the message.

You see, she doesn't really want to. Remember how important marriage is for most girls? Well, going out often means more to them, too. Having a boyfriend of her own means so much that it's hard for her to hear him say he's not really serious. Anyway, who knows. If she sticks around for a while, maybe he'll get serious in time. And anyway, she's a girl – she can't just go off and try another guy. She's got to wait for another guy to ask her. Sure, that's not so likely while she's going out with someone already, but then if she ditches the one she's got, who is going to make sure another one comes around? So she sticks with the one she's got – and that's you!

So, fellows, realize that it's ten to one she's reading more into that invitation than you really mean. Take it carefully or she'll get badly hurt. And girls, don't ask to be hurt. If a fellow says he isn't serious, he means it. So don't let him have you on a string. You're better to keep clear till the serious guy comes along.

Mind you, all this can happen the other way round, too. These days it may be the girl who asks the boy out and he may be wondering how serious she is. It may be he who is in danger of being hurt. But even so, because of the psychology of the two sexes, often it is still the guy who takes the whole business less seriously, and the girl who sees more in it than he does. Then again, many girls don't want the attention of one guy. They just want to be friends with the gang and be left to get on with their career or whatever. And believe it or not, there are many guys who wish the girls would leave them in peace. If you feel like this, whichever sex you are, don't let yourself be rail-roaded into a personal friendship you don't want.

When am I going to talk about starting to go steady? Well, I'm not, because very few people sit down in cold blood and say, 'Right, we're going to go steady now.' They just find out after a while that's what's happened – they've got a steady friend. Looking back it's a bit hard to say just when and how it got that way. This is especially true for people who started going out together rather young. It may be good that way, but it can also mean that the couple drift along together without ever being too sure they are really right for each other. That's another thing that leads to early divorces. Very few marriages go smoothly at the beginning. You have to work at your marriage and you need to want to work at it because you're sure you're right for each other.

The right person?

That leads to a really big question. How do I know that this is the right person for me to marry? Some people go straight to this question without ever going steady, especially if they're older. Some people go steady for quite a while before they suddenly wake up that it's high time they asked the bigger question. It doesn't much matter which way you come to the question; it's one nearly everyone has to answer some time.

There isn't a simple answer to the question either. It's more likely that a successful marriage will result if it is soundly-based. The more it's got going for it, the more it can stand up to the odd thing going the other way. What then are some of the things for and against a couple working out a sound marriage? The most obvious is that we love that person enough, but how do you recognize real love? It's a lot more than just physical attraction – though that may or may not be a start. Some of the best marriages don't start there at all, though they may well finish there in the end.

Here's a handy check-list of ten questions that may help you decide if that friend is really a marriage prospect. Is he or she:

- Someone who shares your basic outlook on life?
- Someone you really honour and respect?
- Someone you trust absolutely?
- Someone you love enough to give yourself to completely, not just in body, but sharing your most private thoughts – the lot?
- Someone you love so much, you couldn't want anyone else later?
- Someone your family can get on with?
- Someone who can share your intellectual life and you theirs; you're not too far apart educationally?
- Someone who shares enough interests for you to have a lot in common?
- A guy who can provide for you satisfactorily or a girl who can run the kind of home you expect?
- Someone who will make the kind of home atmosphere in which you'll be happy to bring up kids?

Many couples won't score 10 out of 10, but if you score less than about seven you're in trouble. Obviously some of the items are vital. How can you make marriage go with someone you don't really trust or who won't make a suitable home for your children?

Christian angles

If you're a Christian, then some of those questions pack an extra punch. For instance, the only kind of person who shares your basic outlook is another Christian and the only person who can give your home a Christian atmosphere is another Christian. That's why Paul wrote what he did about Christians not getting tangled up with non-Christians. Now if you can't marry a non-Christian, there's no future in going out with one either. That's why the questions pack an extra punch.

But then the Christian scores, too, from at least two angles. First of all, if you really take notice of what Jesus said, it gives you standards to live by. When you've got clear standards yourself, you can't help looking at others against those standards. That doesn't mean that you look down your nose at other people saying, 'I'm glad I'm not like him!' In fact you mustn't. But you can't help saying humbly and realistically, '*I'm* not going to be like that.' If you live by firm Christian standards, you aren't likely to get tied up with the wrong kind of girl or guy.

The second thing's a bit harder to make real to someone who's never experienced Christ at work. It's that Jesus promised his Spirit would guide us in life and I've found that's true. He doesn't just give you principles to live by and the strength to do it. He also promises to show you *what* you should do in your life. I know he does it, too; I married the girl I did because I became sure she was God's girl for me. When I'd prayed enough to be sure, I spoke to her about it and you know what she said? 'I've been sure for some time that you are God's choice for me.'

As a matter of fact, to start with I think our relationship was based more on being sure we were for each other than a deep feeling of love. I don't mean that we weren't in love to begin with, because we were. But at that time we didn't know each other very well. Because of the circumstances in which we had been meeting, we'd hardly ever been alone together and you can't love really deeply somebody you hardly know. The love came as we got to know one another and that happened very gradually, because most of our courtship was by the irregular correspondence which was all that my travelling about the remote parts of the world allowed.

We never regretted our rather peculiar courtship. It has proved a thoroughly sound basis for marriage. Like most couples we have found that marriage has its moments. I reckon that getting used to living as close as that to an angel would be tough. I'm no angel and my wife's only one most of the time. When she doesn't appear to be, it is good to lean back and realize that God makes no mistakes. We belong to each other, so let's snap out of it and enjoy what he has given us.

Of course that's how it has happened to work out for us. I hope it will happen quite differently for you from the trans-world courtship angle, but not from the angle of being sure. However it all happens in your life, as a Christian you want to be sure that God leads you in the biggest decision of your life – the person you choose to marry. You won't get too far finding out what God wants you to do if you disobey him and run around with a non-Christian. Nor will you get a green light from God by rushing after one girl (or guy) after another. Just wait and give God time. He will show you what is right, when you're really ready to listen.

5

Unmarried sex

In the last chapter I talked as though between-sex friendships either break up or end in marriage. Actually there are plenty of people who don't break up and they don't get married either. They just have the sex without the marriage. 'And why shouldn't they,' you may ask, 'as long as they're not hurting anybody?'

That suggestion really means something like this. 'Of course it's wrong for married people to mess about. If they do, they hurt the other party; even worse, they hurt the kids. But if it's two single people, well that's different. If they want to go the whole way with sex, what's to stop them? They've got nobody to hurt.' Or have they? What about themselves, for instance?

So let's look at this question of sex outside marriage – and I mean straight sex, not rape or prostitution or homosexuality or any of the other abnormal uses of sex, but just full sexual intercourse with a willing member of the opposite sex. I'm not thinking of married people either; for fairly obvious social and family reasons adultery is a mess. God said the same from the start and history, ancient and modern, proves him right all along the line. So I'm talking about two single people and though that narrows it down a bit, it still leaves us with a stack of different situations to consider.

We'll spell out in chapter six how the Bible says sex is for marriage only, so why not leave it right there? Surely that ought to be good enough for a Christian. Well, it may be, until the situation really hits *you*; then it's different. It's easy to spout Bible principles and believe in them till you find yourself right in the situation. Then you may find you're not so convinced about them after all. That's when it really helps to know that God's standards make sense.

God didn't make a nasty set of tough rules just to spoil our fun, though that's what some people seem to think. No! He made us with sex and his rules are like a maker's manual which tells you how to get the best out of the product. Do it any other way and he won't be held responsible. More than likely you'll get into a real mess. Here are some of the things that can happen!

Casual sex

Let's look first at the idea that sex is just like any other appetite and it does you good to satisfy it now and again. In fact you may get all frustrated if you don't. It sounds fine till you look a bit deeper and realize you are making man like any animal. You can make it sound better by saying 'Sex is just a biological function', but it comes to the same thing. Man is just a body that needs satisfying. Sex is just a few moments of physical passion, enjoyed while they last.

Personally I find that idea of sex pathetic, because it reduces the beautiful human relationship of love to mere biological mating. I know what sex can mean when you really love somebody, so I know how much the 'biological sex' couple are losing. Anyway, if sex isn't really expressing a relationship of love, it's not going to be much good. I've never been with a prostitute, but guys who have tell me you might as well use your hand.

Quite apart from the question of loving, two people need to get to know each other sexually to give each other the full physical pleasure of sex. Casual sex partners never get that far together. But it's the loving bit that really counts. For sex to work really well, you've got to delight in surrendering yourself in love to the other person; you've got to go out to them in deep emotion. That's not going to happen with someone who's just having a cheap sex thrill with you. In fact, the subconscious idea that you're just being used can throw quite a spanner in the works.

This brings us to the key point. Casual sex *does* hurt people. It hurts the people who play it that way, because they are using sex selfishly to give themselves pleasure. Sure, they are giving each other pleasure, too, if both are in it equally, which isn't always the case. Two people are being selfish together, if they have sex without really loving each other and with that selfishness they destroy each other. That's why couples like that can end up hating instead of loving.

It's the psychological bugs in casual sex that are the really big ones and that's why I've discussed them before pregnancy and disease. But these physical problems have to be thought about, too. With Venereal Disease increasing dramatically in spite of modern medicine, you have to face it that casual sex gives you a high risk of infection.

Venereal diseases are nastier than most people realize. 'One shot of antibiotic will fix it' is the general idea. That can be true if you treat the disease straight away and if you don't happen to land an antibiotic-resistant bug. But resistant bugs are increasing and gonorrhoea is so hard to detect in girls, that something like half the girls who've got it don't even know. So they infect guys, who infect other girls ... and so the epidemic rages on. But what's worse, if a girl carries the disease for long, it affects her chances of having children later.

Gonorrhoea is bad enough but syphilis is far worse. You should know all about what syphilis can do to you in the long run.[1] One of its big dangers is that the symptoms can disappear after a time, making you think you've got rid of the disease, when it's working away quietly in you to produce terrible effects later on. It also does terrible damage to the unborn baby of an infected woman.

So, although V.D. can usually be cured if you know you've got it and get the treatment you need, it is still a thing to be reckoned with when you're deciding how you're going to behave with the opposite sex.

Then again a girl doesn't have to get pregnant these days. Many do all the same, which is surprising. You'd think most girls knew how to avoid it. In fact quite a lot don't, but the majority do, and still get

[1] Information can be obtained from the Health Education Council, 78 New Oxford Street, London WC1A 1AH, who publish an information pack *What you Should Know about Sexually Transmitted Infections*. This is also available from your local Health Education Officer, and is free. Information on this subject is usually easily available also at public libraries.

pregnant. The trouble is that the most effective contraception methods[1] involve preparing beforehand for intercourse. A lot of casual sex happens off the cuff and you can't prepare for that. So single girls go on getting pregnant and having abortions or bearing illegitimate children. If you've had anything to do with either, you'll know what a mess it all becomes.

So much hangs on sex that we just have to discipline it. We learn to control all our other emotions and functions. In fact we think people who can't control their temper pretty poor types. It's not really any harder to control love and sex. It's the devil's biggest lie that self-control in sex harms you. Actually it's exactly the other way around; if you don't control your sexual desires, you'll wreck your own life and possibly someone else's, too. That goes whether you're married or not and the trouble is that if you're promiscuous when you're single, who's going to help you kick the habit when you marry? A lot don't and that spells future trouble.

A lot of guys set themselves up with a handy kind of double standard in all this; handy that is, if you can get away with it (and a lot do). They'll have fun with any girl who will give them what they want, and joke and boast about it, too. Using the girl to boost their own sexual ego is about all it amounts to and that's pretty cheap. If you want to get a good laugh, ask the guy if he's interested in marrying the girl. 'What, marry a tart? What do you take me for? When I marry, I'll marry a girl who's decent, thank you.' Now it's your turn to laugh and it's ten to one he

[1] Refer chapter 10.

won't even see why it's funny.

Mind you, it's not only blokes who have double standards. The sex-kitten image makes some girls feel really good and they use men to boost their ego as selfishly as any man uses girls. And they expect to end up with the most decent man in the world – and sometimes appear to succeed! Mostly, of course, it doesn't work out like that because you can't expect more of your partner than you'll give yourself. If you want to marry someone decent they've got the right to someone equally decent in return. If you're going to play around with a whole lot of people who'll end up with somebody else, it's only fair that you take over somebody else's second-hand goods. You can't have it fairer than that, can you?

Expressing love with sex

Right, you say, casual sex like that is pretty low. But that's not the way it is with us. We don't play around casually. We really care about each other; we enjoy being together; we might even get married some day. We like to express our love for each other in all sorts of ways, but we need to express our love in sex to make it really mean something. This isn't sex without a relationship, there is no fear of disease, pregnancy can almost certainly be avoided and it isn't blatantly selfish, so surely it's O.K.?

Well, that *sounds* all right but often it doesn't quite work out that way. The reasons are complicated because relationships vary so much, but here are some things that crop up pretty often, mostly as a result of the different ways men and women look at sex.

Nearly always the suggestion of sex relations comes first from the man. As we've seen, that's natural. He's in love, his sexual urges are aroused and he longs to satisfy them. There's a selfish element in that of course, but it's not only that. He longs to give sexual expression to his love. The chances are the girl doesn't feel quite the same; she's probably pretty scared of giving in sexually. That's partly for fear of becoming pregnant but not only that. Deep down psychologically sex with no prospect of children leaves her only partly satisfied. Then why does she give in to the guy? Perhaps she's scared of losing him. Perhaps it's just that she loves him and gives him what he wants, even though she'd rather not. It could be anything.

But it is right there that the trouble starts. Even though her love makes her willing to give the guy what he wants, subconsciously she knows he's being selfish. Sometimes she registers consciously that he's put his own desires first and either ignored her feelings or, more probably, been too thick to realize how she felt. But if he really loved her, surely he *would* realize. So confidence is undermined, doubt comes in, respect isn't as great as it was and slowly the delight goes out of it all: In time even the sex bit becomes routine and by then it's all rather a mess. The relationship isn't working as it is and yet where else can they go? If they get married what does that alter? They can't get back the first thrills of sex that give so much to the couple who approach marriage fresh. Staying as they are solves nothing and yet splitting up will hurt, too.

It's not always that way, of course. Sometimes the girl really does want the sex part as much as the guy.

She's absolutely happy about it; she starts the pill (or whatever) to make sure she doesn't get pregnant and sets out to enjoy her love affair to the hilt. Yet somehow, after a while, it isn't so good any more. It's the same with a young married couple who delay having children too long. The sexual nature of the woman kicks back from deep inside her. It may show up physically, psychologically or in other odd ways, or it may just lead to sex being gradually less satisfying for her.

Which all leads to the question, where are a couple like that at? If they really care and want to belong to each other, why don't they tell society by getting married? Then they can be fully satisfied and have children. Then they don't have to act as though they are married when they're not, with all the pretences and frustrations that their situation leads to. If they don't really intend to stay together, then in the end what's in it? Just getting badly hurt. That's what often happens. So the designer did have the most clues, after all. Of course, you may be the one out of ten who gets away with it, but you're taking a big risk.

To be complete I must add a word about the couple who believe in life-long partnership but who can't see why it has to be legal marriage. They intend to stay together and raise a family; they may call themselves Mr. and Mrs. for the sake of family and neighbours. But not for them the fuss of a legal ceremony; their marriage is just a private contract. Well, as chapters two and six explain, that's not in line with the facts. There are two main snags about this romantic 'stay together because we want to' idea.

Firstly, in the eyes of the law, the woman is *de facto* and the children are illegitimate. That has tricky legal complications if the man dies or clears out, though a clever will can avoid some of the death problems. All the same it's a tough situation for the children who had no say in the set-up. The second thing comes from the bit about no marriage running smoothly all the time. It's just as well there's a legal hitch to hold people together through patches like that; it makes them work for a solution instead of throwing it all away. The *de facto* couple just don't have that protection from their own bad patches.

Before marriage

There's one other important angle. What about a couple who have been going steady for a while? They've made up their minds to get married soon, so they really do belong to each other. Is there any reason for holding off sex any longer? It becomes especially pressing once a couple are engaged. Then people give them lots of time alone and sexual desires get pretty strong. Why not?

The same question of mutual trust and respect is the first thing that comes up. If the guy can't or won't control his desires before marriage, can the girl really trust him to afterwards? Can the guy completely respect and honour a girl who'll give herself to him when she really feels she shouldn't? We haven't thought much about conscience so far and perhaps we should have, because it does apply all through what we've covered so far. Sexual faithfulness is an idea that runs right through our culture, whether you're a Christian or not. You can't just toss it out and say, 'It's just what we've been conditioned to.' Even if that's so, the fact is that we're all conditioned that way and you can't drown out the voice of your guilty conscience by shouting loudly about hangovers from the past. It doesn't matter where you got it from, your guilty conscience is a real block on satisfactory sex, because it won't let you relax and enjoy it.

The idea of the engagement period is to give a couple the feel of being publicly committed to each other without being legally tied. It tests the relationship to see if it will stand up. If it doesn't, then the engagement can be broken. That will be painful, but it won't be nearly as bad as marriage to the wrong person and possible divorce. Going the whole way sexually during engagement commits the two to each other totally on the physical side. That makes it harder to go back and, if you have to, you are left with memories and feelings which are going to stay with you. It won't be easy to start again with someone else as though you'd never had sexual relations before.

In other words, sex during engagement gets you nowhere and risks a lot. Some people say that you've got to try the sex angle out to make sure you suit each other, but that's tripe. Actually it's worse than tripe – it's dangerously wrong. The first few months of marriage are often the most difficult sexually. The man has to learn to hold and the girl to give. It takes a lot of patient practice to make sexual relations work well all the time. A few experiments before marriage, with feelings of guilt, fear and the rest, may well work out badly. That won't set the marriage up well and it might break the engagement.

No! It's a fact that marriage is three-sided (personal, social and economic) and all three need to go together. To be really satisfactory the sexual relationship needs the personal, social and economic security of a legal marriage.

Delayed reactions

Right now I'm trying to help a girl who's a complete psychological mess. Why? Because she's found out her parents were married only five months before she was born – that's why. I guess she's right in thinking they had to get married because she was on the way. She's convinced they didn't really want to get married and they didn't really want her at all. Worse still she's convinced they don't really love her now, but her much younger brother is adored.

Of course, all teenagers go through the persecution stage, when they're picked on and the other one's the favourite. But you try telling Sue that! No, she's always been the unwanted one and right now she certainly acts that way. It's not going to be easy to change the situation either. Even allowing for Sue's vivid imagination, clearly the parents don't communicate well with each other or with the kids. Even if they did, a total stranger can't waltz into the home and say to them 'Tell your daughter you wanted to conceive her, will you?' Anyway, the dates being what they are, how can they prove it?

Get the point? Your sexual actions now can well kick back viciously, years later, on the life you bring into being. Is it worth it? Is it fair?

The Christian angle

So far this chapter's been mainly plain common

sense, psychological sense perhaps. It's the sort of thing I find myself saying to anybody, Christian or non-Christian. The only special Christian angle is that this common sense is what God said anyway. It all adds up to – obey the maker's instructions and you'll get the thing to work as it should.

When the Christian talks about loving people, he doesn't mean something that's the opposite of love in the sex sense. He just means something bigger, big enough to cut sex down to its proper size. He obeys God, about sex or anything else, not because he's too scared not to, but because he wants to show how much he loves God. Sex outside marriage would not be real love. It would not be doing what is the very best for that person, nor would it be doing what God asks.

A Christian guy can't see a girl as a mere sex object and play with her. She's a person; a person whom God loves and Jesus died for. Anyway her body belongs to somebody – the guy she'll marry some day – and it would be stealing that person's property to take possession of it. Paul actually compares lust to coveting, which is looking with greedy eyes at something that isn't yours. That's not love!

Finally a Christian has got God's picture of marriage to go by and knows that's what sex is really about. It's not going to be worth spoiling that in any way. It's just one more way in which any Christian has to wait for God to unroll his plan in his own good time. Take it from me, that's worth waiting for.

6

So God said it first

There are a lot more sex problems we will have to think about, but the time's come to draw a few threads together first and sew them up a bit. As we've looked at marriage and sex, I've quoted quite a lot from the Bible. I've done that so that you can see it's not just my opinion, but what God said from the start. Now let's bring those various scattered ideas together and have a quick run down on the main Bible principles to do with sex.

There's a lot about sex in the Old Testament (we'll call it the O.T. from here on to save space). The O.T., remember, isn't just one book. It consists of 39 different books, written by many different Jewish authors over a period of at least 1200 years. When the first book was being finished the Jews were a tribe wandering in the desert. Four hundred years later they had a sophisticated kingdom in Palestine, while at the end of the time they were part of the highly developed Graeco-Roman world. Naturally things changed a lot in all that time.

So the O.T. unfolds a gradual development of teaching about everything – God, worship, human society and behaviour. Its teaching about sex unfolds gradually, too, and you can't just take one story or one bit of teaching and say 'there's what the O.T.

teaches about sex'. Taking proof-texts from any part of the Bible like that can land you in a mess. It's how some of the odder sects manage to prove almost anything out of the Bible. You need the whole picture to get the truth of what the Bible teaches and when you get that whole picture it really makes you think.

The Old Testament picture

The O.T. sees marriage as a social, economic and sometimes a political contract. It is also a personal relationship, in which sex expresses the love between a man and a woman, which society recognizes by the institution of marriage. Stories like those of Abraham and Sarah, Isaac and Rebekah and Jacob and Rachel, to name just three, make it clear that love between these couples was a big thing – a whole relationship of which sex was just one part. In the normal course this relationship will lead to the birth of children, but the O.T. does not suggest that procreation is the only purpose of sex. On the other hand it sees little scope for sex outside marriage. Jewish parents were forbidden to allow their daughters to be prostitutes and prostitution is strongly disapproved, even though it did happen.

Adultery (sexual intercourse by a married person with someone other than the marriage partner) is forbidden in the seventh commandment.[1] It is seen in the O.T. as a most serious crime, punishable with death. Jewish society was entirely male-dominated, so that it was common for the woman to get the blame and be punished, as we find in a story in John's

[1] Exodus 20.14.

gospel. [1]. However, the principle is very clear and for good reason. Adultery destroys family life and the whole Jewish society rested on family life even more than do most societies. Jewish religion was a family one, Jewish land was allocated by families and so on. Stable family life was therefore vital for national stability.

There was hardly any scope for sexual intercourse between unmarried people – 'fornication' is the old word for this. The O.T. taught that if any man had intercourse with a virgin, he had to marry her. If he had a wife already, well then he now had a second one as well! In other words, the act of intercourse was regarded as entering into a marriage bond. This was one of the ways in which polygamy developed in O.T. times.

The O.T. nowhere actually forbids polygamy, but it does show that God's plan was for one man to have one wife. That's one of the things in the Adam and Eve story, whether you believe in it literally or not. Then there are many stories of the unhappiness that polygamy leads to. The strife between Jacob's sons, [2] or in David's palace 800 years later [3] are two examples. Read the story of Elkanah's two wives [4] and you get the personal angle of how two wives of the same man don't find it too easy to live together. The O.T. is certainly no sales talk for polygamy.

Although sex is pictured mainly as part of marriage, the O.T. isn't ashamed about sex. Solomon's

[1] John 8.1–11.
[2] Genesis 37.
[3] 2 Samuel 13, 15; 1 Kings 1, 2.
[4] 1 Samuel 1.

Song, for example, in beautiful poetry frankly sings about the beauty of sexual love. Through the O.T. we get the idea that sex, properly used, is one of God's great gifts to mankind, but on the other hand sex misused leads to all the kinds of unhappiness we know today – depression, tension, guilt, family break-ups and, in extreme cases, murder.

The teachings of Jesus

Jesus only said a little about sex but that little lifts the whole subject to a new level. He takes the O.T. as his starting point, saying that he came to make all its laws come true. Then he went on, 'The laws of Moses said, "You shall not commit adultery". But I say: Anyone who even looks at a woman with lust in his eyes has already committed adultery with her in his heart.'[1] And it's no good saying 'Oh, I'm just interested in an example of female beauty for art's sake.' God knows exactly what you're really thinking. Later on the Jews argued about what defiled a person. Jesus was very straight. 'Don't you see that anything you eat passes through the digestive tract and out again? But evil words come from an evil heart and defile the man who says them. For from the heart come evil thoughts, murder, adultery, fornication, theft, lying and slander.'[2] The O.T. treated sex on the level of actions and behaviour. Jesus makes purity a question of attitude and outlook and of course he is right. How you think and feel determines how you act.

John tells us a fascinating story in which Jesus brings out the same point and then makes another

[1] Matthew 5.27, 28, Living Bible.
[2] Matthew 15.17–19, Living Bible.

very important one. As Jesus was teaching a crowd in the temple, the Jewish leaders brought him a woman who had been caught in the act of adultery. 'Moses says we should stone her to death,' they said. 'What do you say?' They were trying to trap him, of course. If he said, 'Don't,' then they could have said he was going against one of the basic O.T. commandments. But if he said, 'Yes, kill her,' they could report him to the Roman authorities as a rebel because the Jews weren't allowed to execute people. How did Jesus answer? 'Whichever one of you has committed no sin may throw the first stone at her.'[1]

Again Jesus is saying, 'Look at yourself inside; that's where sin really happens.' But very subtly he's doing something else, too. He doesn't actually say to them, 'How come you only brought the woman? Did she commit adultery on her own?' He just asks the men who brought her, which one of them is perfectly pure? He was saying to male-dominated Jewish society: there are two sides of sex, male and female, and both sides have their responsibilities. This point is taken up and developed in the letters of the New Testament.

The New Testament Letters

These letters were written mainly by Paul to Christians living in the big Greek cities of the Roman Empire. Sexual customs there were quite different from those of the Jews and also from our own today. The Greek and Roman worlds were totally male-dominated, too, but their sexual standards were nothing like as strict as those of the Jews. Respectable

[1] John 8.1–11.

women were expected to be sexually pure, but generally speaking nobody expected that of a man. He could seek his pleasures where he wanted. I mention this so that you will appreciate that Paul's teaching must have been quite a shock to the typical Greek man.

Paul takes up both the key points Jesus made and develops them into the picture of Christian marriage and *mutual* responsibility which is the subject of the next chapter. He also lays down an approach to sexual behaviour and attitudes which can be briefly summed up as follows:

(a) *Adultery is wrong*
Adulterers are twice warned[1] that they will not inherit God's kingdom. Another letter says that God will judge the immoral and the adulterous.[2] Clearly this kind of behaviour is out for the Christian.

(b) *Other sex outside marriage is wrong*
Paul speaks especially strongly about a Christian who goes with a prostitute. 'You know that your bodies are parts of the body of Christ. Shall I take a part of Christ's body and make it part of the body of a prostitute? Impossible! Or perhaps you don't know that the man who joins his body to a prostitute becomes physically one with her? The scripture says quite plainly, "The two will become one body" ... Avoid immorality. Any other sin a man commits does not affect his body; but the man who commits immorality sins against his own body. Don't you know that your body is the Temple of the Holy Spirit,

---

[1] 1 Corinthians 6.9, 10; Galatians 5.19.
[2] Hebrews 13.4.

who lives in you, the Spirit given you by God? You do not belong to yourselves but to God; he bought you for a price. So use your bodies for God's glory.'[1]

The principle Paul states obviously applies more widely and in a lot of other letters[2], sexual immorality of all kinds figures in the lists of sins which Christians will avoid. If this sounds rather negative, don't forget that God made sex in man. He knows how he intended it to work and how people can make a mess of what he intended. It would hardly be kind if he didn't tell us what to avoid! Fortunately that isn't all he does; he also gives us some very positive ideas.

(c) *Be clean in thought, word and action*
Jesus lifted sex from action to thought. James develops that idea, 'But a person is tempted when he is drawn away and trapped by his own evil desire; then his evil desire conceives and gives birth to sin; and sin, when it is full-grown, gives birth to death.'[3] Paul points out that we need to be clean in thought and word, as well as in action, when he says, 'Since you are God's people, it is not right that any questions of immorality, or indecency, or greed should even be mentioned among you. Nor is it fitting for you to use obscene, foolish, or dirty words. Rather you should give thanks to God. You may be sure of this: no man who is immoral, indecent, or greedy will ever receive a share in the Kingdom of Christ and of God.'[4]

(d) *Be kind, considerate and thoughtful*
In chapter two I referred to Paul's marvellous picture

[1] Corinthians 6.15–20.
[2] Colossians 3.5; 1 Thessalonians 4.3.
[3] James 1.14, 15.
[4] Ephesians 5.3–5.

of marriage from Ephesians chapter 5. The famous chapter on love in 1 Corinthians 13 is another of the many passages which hammer home to the Christian that he or she is to be kind and considerate to everyone. We are all good at applying that to others but not so good at fitting it to ourselves, especially in our home relationships. This is one of the most positive ways in which Christ helps marriage. If he rules your life, you'll be such a better person to live with!

So!

So the Christian standard is high. It's got its negative side, the things best to avoid, and it's got a strong positive side, the good things you should aim for. The Christian standard applies right through to the end of married life from the first days of interest in the other sex. So let's apply it next to the friendship and courting stages.

7

How far can you go?

If sexual intercourse is out, then how far can you go on the physical side? Now that's a tough one. There isn't one simple answer. It all depends on the set-up. You go into a group you hardly know, pick the best-looking girl, sweep her into your arms, and plant a passionate kiss on her lips – well, that's too far and you could easily find yourself on an assault charge. But you come home after being overseas for six months, and your fiancée's there to meet you at the airport. Just go and shake hands with her and see what you get! That's not far enough!

So where does that get us? Is it really true that 'How we ought to behave *all* depends on the situation?' That idea is fine if you leave the word 'all' out, but leave it in and you land in the situation ethics quagmire, where you can do anything at all as long as it's done out of love. The way the 'law of love' is worked out by Hugh Heffner in Playboy magazine certainly gives you plenty of scope. Whether sex is right or wrong doesn't have anything to do with who's married to whom; it's just a question of what helps someone to feel better at the time.

Now the Christian can't go along with that. This may be the 20th century, we may be educated, enlightened, liberated and the rest, but right is still right and wrong is still wrong. God has set up a high standard and it is worth living by. It isn't only a question of avoiding sex outside marriage. That would be very negative. Christianity is positive; it's about the way you think and your whole attitude to sex and people. That makes it quite searching.

Is love everything?

Jesus' golden rule for behaviour between people was 'love' – just where situation ethics starts, too. How come they work out so differently? The answer's quite easy. In situation ethics loving other humans is the only thing; for Jesus, loving people is only the *second* golden rule of life. He put another rule before it – that you love God above everybody else.[1] That keeps the other rule on the track.

To explain how two ideas of love can start out much the same and end up so differently, imagine that two people start out for the same rendezvous a few miles northward in really tangled country. They start off in the same direction all right, but they strike a cliff directly in the way. A decides to detour to the west and he finds it a bit rugged, but once he is out of that he's fine. He pulls out his compass, lines up north, and heads there. B goes around the cliff eastwards and finds quite an easy route. He hasn't got a compass but, having a fair idea of the lie of the land, he's not worried. He wishes the sun would come out so that he can check his line but the cloud won't let him, so he just swings back northwards and heads that way. He's not far off in his sense of direction either, but ten small hills and three gullies later he's

[1] Mark 12.30, 31.

not so sure. He hopes he's right, though actually he's heading south-east. All that swing has come about from a series of little changes in direction which he didn't really notice.

You get the point? Without some other standard to guide it, the law of love is all relative and it can land you just about anywhere. Jesus' first rule (to love God) is like a compass to keep a Christian's love on track. Really loving and caring is basic for the Christian and God's love shows us how.

Real love and care

It's hard to know where to start applying that kind of love to relations between the sexes. There's so much in it and I have already discussed some of the problems – like that of being easy to live with. What's more, the Christian man won't look on a girl as a sex object. If God sees male and female equally as people, there won't be any room for a double standard either. There's a general idea that it's O.K. for a guy to go as far as the girl will let him. It's her job to say no, isn't it? In a sense, of course it is. She's the one who will get pregnant, so she takes the rap. She has to say no to protect herself, but that's all wrong from a Christian angle. It's saying that God has two sets of rules, an easy one for men and a tough one for girls.

Well, that's just not on. God sees everyone the same way and he expects everyone to live to the same standard. A Christian guy is expected to have the same control over his sex drives as a Christian girl is. Really the man has the bigger responsibility for self-control, because he is usually the one who pushes the sex side along. He can't lumber the girl with the job of controlling him as well as herself. Two Christians will accept an equal share of the responsibility for how to behave together and for keeping everything on the level.

Love is two-sided in all its aspects; it's mutual and neither is going to take advantage of the other. That means neither will just string the other along and play with their affections without being serious. The man won't get the girl in a corner and take advantage of her sexually and the girl won't take advantage of the man's sexual drives to lead him on, which is another way of saying she'll dress and act decently – the old word is 'modestly'.

The New Testament says quite a lot to girls about modesty, which musn't be confused with fashion. No doubt clothing can get so brief that modesty isn't possible, but a girl covered from neck to ankle can be immodest, too. So modesty is partly a question of dress, but it's really more one of behaviour. It isn't square; it's just sensible and it's absolutely required of Christians. Remember, too, girls, you don't reduce your prospects by being modest. Rather the reverse, in fact. The easy-come girl may create a bit of a stir, but most fellows find a modest girl more attractive as a person.

Among other things, a girl who's immodest is embarrassing; embarrassing to the guy she's with, to her friends, to the group and to strangers. She's not acting considerately to any of them and that's a good test of whether you're being truly loving, both for guys and girls. I remember a couple in a great group of teenagers – a clean, decent group who really cared about each other. They came to supper at our place now and again and this couple came, too. While everyone else acted delightfully naturally, this girl would drape herself all around the guy. Sure it was a squash but no one else found it that crowded! He couldn't keep his hands off her and I found it really embarrassing. So did everybody else. Some of them were really mad about it and were glad when the couple stopped coming. That kind of behaviour isn't loving; its just plain inconsiderate.

Courting and married couples can be thoughtless and selfish in the same kind of way. They are so happy together, so thrilled about it all, that they love to show everyone how much they love each other. O.K., fine – up to a point. But the chances are that in any mob of youth there are others who'd just love to have a special friend of the opposite sex and haven't got one yet. If you're like that and sore about it inside, it really hurts to have a couple throw their love and pleasure at you all the time. Such selfish pairing-up is a curse in a lot of church groups. As a Christian, remember, you have to care about everyone.

When is it sex?

Now let's think how a couple's behaviour affects not other people but themselves. They're in love, or think they are, and they want to show each other how they feel, physically. How far can they go? Well – this is where we began the chapter – that obviously depends on the set-up.

First, let's get something straight. Kissing (I don't mean a peck), cuddling, handling each other's bodies in any way are all sexual acts. That doesn't mean there's anything wrong about them in the right place;

it just means that they have a specific purpose – to stir you both up to greater sexual desire and prepare your bodies for sexual intercourse. The Christian has to be absolutely pure about sex and this includes all sexual acts, however simple.

I've had members of church youth groups tell me it's O.K. to neck and pet as long as they don't actually go the whole way to sexual intercourse. (Necking usually means handling each others' bodies generally, while heavy petting involves handling each others' sex parts.) Apart from the fact that you can't just say 'stop there' as easily as all that, for the Christian it's wrong. It's using sex for selfish pleasure and it's toying with the body of somebody who may not belong to you. Any Christian guy has to ask himself, before he puts a hand on a girl, 'Does she belong to me – and not just for this week?' Any sexual play is sex and on a casual basis, for kicks, it's out!

A growing love

Fair enough, you say, but this isn't casual. I'm dead serious and I've got to start kissing the girl sometime. Of course you have. If you're serious and there's a love-relationship growing up between you, it's natural that the physical side will develop with the rest. The main thing is to keep things in proportion. A love affair is like a three-legged stool, with spiritual, mental and physical 'legs' to support it. If one is twice as long as the other two, it won't be much good as a stool, or a love affair! Taking the physical side way ahead of the rest just throws the whole relationship out of balance and asks for trouble.

There is no simple answer to the courting couple

who ask, 'How far can we go?' The sexual conduct of two people is an entirely personal thing between themselves and, if they are Christians, between the two of them and God. They'll want to keep their consciences clear and their relationship with God straight. Anything that makes self-control difficult obviously won't help to do that. A clear conscience before God is one guide to sensible behaviour.

There's another angle, too. Anyone who's had a long engagement will tell you what a strain it becomes. It's not so bad if you're separated by distance but, if you're seeing each other all the time, you feel more and more that you belong to each other. You do everything together all day and then at night go to your separate rooms. Inevitably you get to saying, 'What's the point? It's time we slept together, too.' Fine! So you're ready to be married! And if you can't be, then the greater is the physical intimacy when you're together, and the more frustrating it becomes to have to hold off going the whole way. So a long engagement doesn't solve the problem.

The important thing is to let the whole love relationship unfold gradually and naturally. 'Whole' is the key word – not just one side or other. Really getting to know someone intimately and weaving your life into theirs is a thrill, if you keep everything in balance. If you don't, the relationship won't work out and you'll find in the end that you've played it all wrong. The trouble is that by then it's often too late. So it's best to take it gently.

8

Boss of yourself?

This chapter is about self-control. Some people don't go much on it these days, but for a Christian it's important. So it is for others, too, if they only realized. Anyone training for a sport needs physical and emotional self-control. Watch a tennis star throw a tantrum on the centre court at Wimbledon and you'll see what I mean. To do any tricky job you have to have control of your limbs, hands and especially your fingers. To think a tough problem through you need to control your mind and organize its working to find a solution. Every facet of life needs self-control; without it you get nowhere.

If lack of self-control wrecks almost every other part of life, isn't it odd that a lot of people talk about sex as though it can't be controlled or trying to control it may harm you? How wrong that all is! As we've seen, sex is better controlled. In fact, when you think about the mess lack of control produces, you can't make a decent go of life without control. The question is, how do you achieve it?

Let's begin with some of the things that make control of sex difficult, if not impossible. For example, there's getting into the wrong kind of situation or with the wrong crowd. If you're at a party where everything goes sex-wise, then you're not going to find it easy to keep yourself under control. If you get with a group whose talk is always sex-filled and smutty, then it's going to affect you that way in the end. If a guy fills his mind with magazine pictures of naked girls in sexy poses, or a girl soaks up lurid romance comics by the yard, it doesn't exactly lift your mind, does it?

The battle of the mind

Now Jesus said that sex temptations start in the mind and we all know that's true. That's where the sex battle has to be won, so we have to guard our minds. Paul wasn't talking only about sex when he said, 'Fill your minds with those things that are good and deserve praise: things that are true, noble, right, pure, lovely and honourable,'[1] but I imagine he had it in mind among other things.

You may be thinking, 'But don't psychologists tell us that repressing our sexual desires can do a lot of harm?' They do and they are right. But do you understand repression? Have you ever tried to get a little boy to sit still in silence for five minutes? After 15 seconds he tries to tell you something. You put your fingers to your lips. Almost immediately he wants to scratch. You stop him. He tries to tell you why he needs to. You stop him. Before long he's flicking his fingers, then kicking his legs. Your patience with repressing him will run out long before five minutes is up! But put him in front of *Dr. Who* and tell him to come and get you when he's had enough and he'll sit there glued to the idiot box for a long time.

The one is repression – the other is sublimation,

[1] Philippians 4.8

which has been described as the 'expulsive power of a new affection'. With the Time Lords filling his mind, our little friend doesn't even think of the itch or the need to wag his tongue!

Sublimation is, in fact, the key to sexual control. It isn't exactly 'using up sexual energy in some other way' as I've heard it described. It's so filling your life with worthwhile things that there really isn't too much room for the misuse of sexual powers. That, of course, is exactly what Paul was on about, though he was referring to controlling life as a whole and not just sex.

So Christianity is right on line; it's the battle for the mind that counts. But Jesus didn't just tell you to guard your mind and leave you to get on and do the best you can by yourself. He did far more than that, for he died on the cross and at the Last Supper he told his disciples why he was going to die. He was doing it to make them clean[1] and that offer of forgiveness is still open to people today. Then he said he was going to send someone who'd stay with them and strengthen and keep them.

That happened at Pentecost, the first Whitsunday, when God's Spirit came to the first Christians. He was real power. Take Peter, for example. He'd been so scared of a servant girl that he wouldn't admit to her that he was a follower of Jesus. Yet now he's in the middle of the Jerusalem that crucified Jesus, telling them all what a terrible thing he'd done. When God's Spirit comes into your life, he starts from the inside. He makes you want what is right and hate what is wrong. He's no vague 'it'; he's a real person with

[1] Matthew 26.28.

power to change people for the better.

That's why the Christian has the real answer to sex. When God thinks his thoughts through you it gives you a new slant on everything, including sex. When the Spirit does his job of making Jesus real to you, you find you have a companion and friend who helps to keep your conscience tender. You can't take him into that smutty joke club with you, so you leave him behind or you stay out. The same thing goes for every aspect of sex – thought, talk or action.

Christians have sex problems, too

Don't get the idea, though, that sex is easy to handle just because you're a Christian, because it isn't. As my friend Dave said in chapter one, sex is just as much a problem to Christians as anyone else, and they need to remember that. Occasionally you get a really nasty sex scandal right inside the church circle. People say, 'Tut-tut, however could that happen among Christians?' They've got the idea people are immune from sex temptations because they're Christians. But Christians can get careless and fail to discipline their minds as strictly as they once did. Then they relax on the common-sense rules which most people follow in their behaviour with the opposite sex. They allow unwise intimacies and, before you know where you are, there's immorality and a scandal. It's not very common I'm glad to say, but it happens and that's why.

A person who becomes a Christian stays just as human as someone who doesn't. He still has the same sexual instincts as before. These need just as much controlling, too; the only difference is that the

Christian has God's power in him and that's everything. But having the answer doesn't make the job of control easy – it's just that you know how to go about it. Most Christians find controlling sex is really tough and you have to learn gradually how to let God take control of you. That's what the Christian life's all about – letting God rule your life so that you are firmly under control. [1]

Practical common sense

There's a lot of practical common sense involved in controlling sex, too, whether you're a Christian or not. I've already talked about the kind of group you're in and the magazines you read. Then there are books; a lot of them aren't as sexy as the covers make them look, but there are also plenty that only sell because of the sex bits. What about films and plays, too? They aren't necessarily bad because they've got a sex theme. It's not the theme but the treatment that determines how a film or play affects you. Some really make you think and that can be good; others are just designed to titillate and that's bad.

Even the physical contents of the surrounding atmosphere have sexual repercussions. A warm, cosy room with dim lights and soft music is romantic. It also acts physically on the nervous system to relax you and produce those feelings of intimacy which are a natural basis for sexual activities. Try opening some windows and letting an icy blast through and see how passionate you feel! And little girl, if you really want to see your Romeo's passions disappear, drop an ice

[1] If you want a good book to help you read more about this side, I suggest *The Fight*, by John White (Inter-Varsity Press).

cube down his neck! He'll soon cool off in more ways than one!

Probably the most important thing is the way you let yourself behave with individuals of the opposite sex. Accepted conventions aren't just old fashioned courtesy, which you can ditch as square whenever you like. They have a lot of good sense behind them. Spending a lot of time alone with an opposite-sex friend must affect you; it's a sex situation just because you are of the opposite sex. If she sits very close or he handles her, then inevitably things start from there. Being discreet and correct is just plain common sense really.

Masturbation

There is one control problem of a different kind that needs a bit of thought – the question of masturbation. That means sex on your own, stimulation of your own sex organs leading to orgasm. It is more of a guy's problem, so let's start there. Every normal male knows the urge to help nature get rid of the excess semen which builds up in his body and most do it from time to time. It won't do you any harm physically either, though it's just as good to let nature have its way. A Christian might say that God's natural way is best and that makes anything else second best and, in that sense, wrong.

There are some snags about masturbation, though, in a rather different way. First, in order to masturbate, a guy has to fill his mind with sexy thoughts and that doesn't help a Christian to keep his mind clean and to keep sex under firm control. Secondly, it is a selfish use of sex – just for one's own moment of satisfaction and that's not the real idea of sex at all. The habit of using sex selfishly isn't a good one. It is the very opposite to the unselfish way in which sex should be used in real love.

Some guys, especially those who really want to live God's way, feel all burnt up about masturbation. They feel so guilty, the worst guy in the world. Get it clear that you aren't. I can't honestly say, 'Forget it, it's quite O.K.,' because I've just explained the snags. But I can say, don't make a big thing of it. It's a problem that stops when you get married and have normal sex outlets. Meanwhile, it's a very common and persistent desire over which God's Spirit can win control and make you boss of yourself.

Never having been a girl, I find it harder to write on the other side. You may not have a problem anyway; I know a lot of girls don't strike it, because a girl's bodily cycle has little to do with sexual pleasure. However, more open discussion about all sexual matters, which is a good thing, may lead to an increase in female masturbation because of the natural temptation to experiment. The same snags arise as for guys. Being selfish about sex is just as damaging for a girl. So is filling your mind with the wrong kind of sex thoughts and a girl needs to be in control of herself just as much as a guy does.

The Bible doesn't seem to mention masturbation anywhere. That's probably because it wasn't much of a problem in those days; in Bible times you got married pretty soon after you matured sexually. It's our modern society that has produced the long gap between sexual maturity and marriage, with the consequent problem of sexual control for sexually-mature single people. In the absence of direct teaching, the Christian has to apply general principles to work out how he will run his life and that's what I've tried to do in writing about masturbation.

9

Gone too far?

Most of this book, so far, has talked about how we ought to handle sex and what God, who made sex, says about it and so on. It lays out an ideal pattern and suggests you try and follow it. That's fine for someone who is perfect. Unfortunately that's not me and it's probably not you either. So the chances are that sooner or later you're going to find yourself involved in sex in some way you regret. How do you handle that?

Keep sex in focus

That's the important thing. If you've been brought up in a Christian background, you may find that hard to do. You'll have been conditioned to put sex right at the top of the sin scale and you'll be thinking of yourself as the worst guy in the world because you've come unstuck over sex.

That outlook is pretty common but it's certainly not Christian. Jesus nowhere treated sex as the worst sin. Far from it, in fact. Remember the woman caught in adultery? Jesus took that very calmly. One of the women closest to Jesus, Mary Magdalene, seems to have been a prostitute before she met him and the Jews despised Jesus for his association with 'prostitutes and sinners'.

The rest of the New Testament is the same. It sees sex sins as serious, especially in the church, because they wreck relationships, not just within the family but everywhere. In that way sex sins are on their own, but that's only saying sex sins have their own particular consequences. Jealousy and back-biting wreck relationships as much, but in a different way. Pride and selfishness are just as ugly in their own way. Christian teaching doesn't rate sins at all – they're all bad and basically they all need exactly the same remedy.

Getting straightened out

There are several angles on how to cope with a messy sex situation you've got yourself in. You have to get out of a jam you're in, you need to undo any harm you've done as far as you can, and then you have to get yourself back on track and be able to live with your conscience. Obviously the three tie up together pretty closely. If you've done serious harm to someone, like getting a girl pregnant, you're going to find it hard to live with your conscience, because you can't undo what you've done. Even an abortion doesn't put a girl back to square one, but more of that later.

So what's the answer, then? As a Christian I just have to start from base. I know that Jesus died so that I could be forgiven and he didn't say 'except for sex sins'. He died for *all* my sin, so if I tell him I'm sorry, he'll forgive me. 'O.K.,' you say, 'of course I'm sorry I'm in this jam.' Yes, but that's not what the Bible means at all. You're just sorry for yourself, that's all. If you want God to forgive you, you've got to be sorry not for yourself, but because you've hurt God and the other party and you hate what you've done.

Don't get the wrong idea. The Christian doesn't get himself neatly off the hook by telling God he's sorry so that he can feel better. That might be very convenient but there's far more to the Christian answer than that. If you're truly sorry in the Christian way, you'll want to do all you can to straighten out the mess you've created. But once you've faced where you stand with God, it will be much easier to do the next thing, which is to talk the situation out calmly with the other party. You won't be blaming anyone – except yourself that is – but you'll be working out the situation together, determined to put things right.

You'll also find it easier to talk to some older person. Having put the record straight with God, you don't have to cover up any more. You can face letting someone else see your worst side. I really want to say this loud and clear – finding someone more experienced whose advice you can trust is the best possible thing to do, *whatever* the jam you're in.

Jam number one

So you've gone too far! Oh, you stopped it in time, fortunately, but it went a lot further than you intended. It's put a damper on your friendship, somehow. Is it embarrassment or that you're scared? A bit of both, perhaps, but you've certainly found out for yourself just what a punch the sex thing packs. Well, that's a pretty good lesson to have learnt, as long as you've really learnt it.

Where do you go now? Have you talked the thing out together? No? Then you'll have to. You've got to make up your mind whether you want to go on together or not. If you don't really respect each other after what happened, you'd better break up for a while and see how things work out. In some ways that's the easiest answer.

If you decide, on the other hand, to keep going together, then don't try and pretend nothing ever happened. You have to face that it did and you have to agree on commonsense rules for yourselves, on how often you meet and where. You'll have to be quite practical about keeping the passion bit under control. And watch it; deciding on principles is O.K. but carrying them out will be tough. If you're Christians, be sure you bring God right into this, too. Let it be open between the three of you that you're in it together and that the two of you want your friendship to please him.

Jam number two

So you've gone too far; much too far. It wasn't just a casual slip either. You set out to enjoy your holiday together to the full and the sex was part of the deal. It was a good time, too, but now, looking back on it, you're not too sure. You haven't heard from her (him) in the four days you've been home; perhaps you're not the only one having second thoughts. You ought to make contact and find out, but there's something holding you back, is there? That's natural, of course, because you've changed the whole basis of your friendship and neither of you is quite sure how to handle it now. One thing's sure, though; you can't go back to where things were before.

So what will you do? That depends. If you're

thinking of going right on as you are now, may I ask you to read chapter 5 again very thoughtfully. I can't say any more, can I? But if you want to pull back, man (or girl), you've got a problem. Do you keep going together at all, or don't you? That's the first thing to decide and from there on it's a bit like jam number one, except that everything is just that much more difficult.

There's one other thing. Some Christians take the line that, in God's eyes, you're married to the first person you have sex with. That follows, in a way, from the Old Testament rule that a man had to marry any virgin he seduced. The first experience of physical love is, no doubt, something very special for most people and a memory that sticks with you, but I don't see where the Bible spells out that it's the same as marriage. Marriage is far more than sex. It would be terrible to spend life married to the wrong person just because you got trapped into having sex together.

Jam number three

You've guessed it! This is where we came in in chapter one. She's (you're) pregnant, so what now? In all normal circumstances there is one thing you have to do – tell the parents, on both sides. It applies to the girl's parents however old she is, as she'll need the support of a home whatever happens. Unless the guy is fully independent of his parents, he'll be very wise to tell them. Then go and see someone outside both families, who can advise and help you. You may prefer to do that first, in fact.

The first reactions of both families may well be that

you'd better get married – quick. Don't let them rush you into that, because it may not be the best answer. Shot-gun marriages have a higher chance of failure than the average, for the reasons we've talked about already. What you've got to do is to work out together whether you really would have wanted to get married if this hadn't happened. If you're sure you would have, if you're sure you haven't lost respect for each other, then certainly the best solution is to go right ahead and get married. But don't forget the story of Sue at the end of chapter five. That's a problem to face *before* you marry, not when 'your' Sue's old enough to ask how come she was born six months after you got married.

But if you're not pretty sure, then you're taking a very big risk going ahead and you may be better to look at the other alternatives. This may mean resisting family pressure and that's where an older person outside the family can really help.

But what if you don't get married? Well the important thing is to realize there is no way back to square one. There are three choices before the girl, or hopefully the two of you together, and none of them turns the clock back to before she became pregnant – not even an abortion, which I'll come to in chapter ten. The question of whether abortion is right in such circumstances is a very difficult one. Most Christians are very much against it as I'll explain then. All I want to say here to any pregnant girl is not to listen to or get involved with amateurs. If you need an abortion it can be arranged legally and pro-fessionally. But be sure to talk to your doctor privately and you may be wise to talk, too, with a psychologist with experience in the abortion field.

That leaves the alternative of having the baby. These days, happily, very few families take the line of throwing a pregnant daughter out. Whatever your parents may say at first – they'll probably say plenty till they get over the shock and you mustn't mind – they'll probably stand right behind you and that will take a great load off you. You can then work out with them how to handle it all.

Whatever you do, don't let shame or fear or some such reason make you run away from home and try and cope on your own. You won't be able to. You can't stay in your job right through and you'll need support. If by any chance your home won't stand behind you, there are quite a number of organizations who will help you. Get your doctor to put you in touch with one of them. To the guy I have to say – you have to stand by too and provide the money needed to see the girl through this time. There's nothing so low as the guy who just dumps the girl he's got pregnant.

Of course, there's still one big question to be answered – whether to keep the baby or not. It's a terribly hard one and I think each girl has to make her own decision. She has to think of the child's future as well as her own and in many cases adoption offers the child the better future. I think the important thing is to make up your mind well before the baby is born and to be sure to stick to it. Immediately after bearing a child is no time to have to make a big decision about anything.

A serious social problem is developing because girls don't decide beforehand. After the baby is born a girl's strong maternal instincts make her want to feed and care for her child. While the baby is small it works out quite well, but not for very long. Two years later she has a hard-to-manage toddler of two on her hands – around her neck, in fact, because she now sees how hard it is for a mother of a child of two to find a husband. By the time it is all over, another disturbed three-year-old is out for adoption.

On the whole, then, adoption offers the child the better bet. It isn't so easy for the mother. Some girls seem to put the whole episode behind them quite well. Others don't. They just can't control that motherly instinct which wonders about the child they have borne. Deep down they feel despised and this feeling keeps kicking back at them psychologically for years. That is why the decision is such a hard one to make. Every road forward from an unwanted pregnancy has snags.

One final thing. However serious the sex jam you've got in, God cares as much as ever about you. However bad you feel, you can be sure of his forgiveness on the terms I've told you. That doesn't take away the pregnancy, but it puts you right with the greatest power of all and he can see you through any time, however tough.

10

Contraception
and abortion

In this chapter I want to tackle two subjects which aren't mentioned in the Bible and over which Christians disagree.

Contraception

The word 'contraception' means preventing pregnancy from sexual intercourse. A contraceptive is something which does this. There are two quite separate things to talk about; first, whether contraception is right or wrong and, secondly, how it works.

Some Christians get very uptight when single people are told how contraceptives work, for fear it encourages them to have sex. I agree that more single people probably go the whole way now that there are pretty effective contraceptives. However, I've explained in chapter five that the risk of pregnancy is only a small part of the argument against sex outside marriage. If, in spite of all those arguments, two people are going to have sexual intercourse, then I think it's better that they know how to avoid getting into a pregnancy problem on top of all the rest of the trouble they're heading for. So here goes!

For and against

Some church leaders have taken a stand against contraception. They oppose all 'artificial' contraception on theological arguments about sex which I find hard to follow but with which I think I disagree. This book isn't the place for that kind of argument. Personally I'm sorry church leaders make a theological issue out of a subject the Bible says nothing about directly. They seem to be making rules about private aspects of people's lives which individual couples should be free to decide for themselves.

The most common Christian view seems to be something like this. The control of the world's population is now a major problem. In the underdeveloped countries it's essential to prevent mass starvation. In the developed countries it's just as essential, because we use so much of the world's resources and produce so much of the global pollution. What's more the health situation in developed countries is so good that very few babies die. Therefore, it is essential to prevent too many being conceived.

Now there are only two methods of doing this. One is to stop having sexual intercourse. The other is to use some method of contraception. While short periods of abstaining from sex don't hurt at all, psychologists and marriage counsellors all agree that long abstinence within marriage is likely to damage the marriage and affect the people concerned. Paul says exactly the same in 1 Corinthians 7.1–5. Therefore, the responsible Christian couple will use contraceptive methods to plan their family in accordance with what they feel God wants them to do.

Contraceptive methods
There are three main types of contraception. The first type is usually called '*natural*' because it is based upon understanding and observing a woman's natural menstrual cycle. [1]

The old 'rhythm' method depended on predicting the beginning of a woman's next period and then using the so-called 'safe week' before that for intercourse. This method had two big snags. Very few women have such regular periods that the prediction was reliable and it restricted intercourse to the one week of the month when a woman's sexual desires are least strong.

There are now two much better natural methods which make it possible to pinpoint the time of ovulation accurately. The 'ovulation' method involves watching the mucus which is produced in a woman's vagina. This mucus changes before ovulation in a way which is quite easy to recognize once the woman has been taught in a Family Planning clinic. She then knows the days before and after ovulation when she is not fertile.

The 'temperature' method uses the fact that a woman's temperature before she gets up in the morning rises slightly after ovulation. So she can work out for sure when, after ovulation, she will not be fertile. It does not tell her anything about the time before ovulation.

We might call the second type of contraception the *mechanical* type. It consists of various methods of putting a mechanical obstacle in the way of fertilization or implantation. The simplest is the sheath or

[1] See chapter three.

'french letter' which is placed over the man's penis before he enters the vagina. It is very convenient for the one-shot occasion and requires no premeditation, beyond being sure you have one available. However, many couples find it unsatisfactory to have to interrupt the lovemaking process to put the sheath on. It also means that the male and female organs are not in physical contact and this seriously affects the pleasure for many people.

A more satisfactory mechanical device is a rubber cap which can be inserted by the woman in the vagina, so as to cover the opening of the womb, thus preventing sperms entering. The cap is usually coated with a spermicidal preparation as well. It has the advantage that it can be inserted at any time beforehand, and if properly fitted, neither party is conscious of it at all. However, initial fitting requires a medical examination and the woman must anticipate intercourse and insert the cap beforehand.

The third mechanical method does not prevent conception but prevents the fertilized egg being implanted in the womb. It consists of a small sterile coil or loop inserted in the womb by a doctor. This appears to be quite harmless but can cause enough irritation to prevent implantation. These intrauterine devices, as a cheap and effective method, are favoured for underdeveloped countries but are also common in Australia. The main disadvantage is that quite a lot of women cannot retain the device but spontaneously expel it. It also requires a doctor to insert the device and to remove it when a further pregnancy is planned.

The remaining broad type of contraceptive is

pharmaceutical – the pill in other words. It works by changing the oestrogen level in a woman's body just enough to prevent ovulation. By interrupting the treatment and taking pills with no hormone in them for a few days, a somewhat shorter menstrual period is allowed to occur. The method is easy and fairly certain and very popular indeed in Australia. The main disadvantage is that most of the present pills produce side effects in many women. This is why the pill requires a medical prescription. Even if you can get it on the side, it's not a safe thing to do. There is still argument about how long you can go on taking the pill safely. Most doctors currently recommend young marrieds not to use it for more than two years because fertility seems to drop if you do.

The unmarried couple

All this explains why contraceptives don't help too much to stop casual sex causing pregnancy. The best and safest need medical prescription or fitting. The sheath is about the only one available for the couple making love casually and a lot don't bother or find it unsatisfactory. Of course, two single people who are going to live together can plan contraception in the same way as a married couple and they certainly should. Contraceptives enable them to be pretty sure of avoiding pregnancy but, as I've said, that's only a small part of their problem.

Abortion

As I start to write this section, I have the feeling that, whatever I say, I'm in trouble with somebody! I've just read again a collection of articles by a string of

Christian experts in every field. All they really prove is that it's a very difficult subject about which the Bible says nothing directly.

When a Christian finds himself in this sort of situation he has to look for a related Bible principle and try to apply that. In this case the most obvious principle is that it is wrong to take a human life. But applying that principle leads to a new question: When does the unborn child become human? Before that point, abortion is not killing a human being.

Many theologians feel the answer is quite clear. They take the line that the foetus is fully human from the moment of conception. The foetus has a 'right to life', they say, just as much as you and I have, so that makes all abortion into murder.

At the other extreme are people who say that a baby is human only when it becomes independent of its mother's life, that is when it has been born. Abortion, therefore, is not murder and is allowable at any time, provided no other principle rules against it in a particular case. This view runs into the snag that a baby is fully developed, except in size, two months before birth and could live on its own if it had to, as in the case of a premature birth or the death of the mother in an accident.

There are various views between the two extremes, but they all have to try and fix some recognizable point in the ante-natal process when the foetus becomes human. Most commonly people choose the time of 'quickening', when the movement of the foetus is first felt by the mother. This corresponds roughly with the three-month point favoured in most abortion law reform proposals. But this idea has snags to it, too, as it makes the mother's sensations decide whether a foetus is human or not.

Personally I doubt whether there is much point in the whole argument about when a foetus becomes truly human. It seems to be looking for black and white answers where there aren't any. It all seems to assume that we only have to choose between good and bad. But real life isn't like that. It's not only black and white; it's every shade of grey in between. Often a choice is not between good and bad but between something bad and something worse. When pregnancy endangers an expectant mother's life there are two choices only and both are unhappy. Either take the life of the foetus or risk that of the mother.

Here's another sticky one. A young married couple are expecting their second child. Early in the pregnancy the wife gets German measles and her doctor warns her that there is a high risk of the child being born defective in some way. In view of the fact that the couple are young and should be able to have as many more children as they want, he advises an abortion. Is it wrong for the couple to consider it on the score that it would be murder of the unborn infant? Or is it irresponsible knowingly to risk bringing a defective child into the world? This is no black and white case. It's real life, a choice perhaps between two undesirable courses. Obviously each couple must answer to God for themselves but I have no doubt what I think. In such a case abortion should be seriously considered. But, even if an abortion of this kind *is* performed, the advice to such couples (as to those who have recently experienced a miscarriage) should be, 'Try again, quickly.'

Of course, today's debate about abortion is not mainly about the kind of situation I've described. It's mostly about single girls who get pregnant. If a single girl can't satisfactorily rear a child and if having the baby adopted produces psychological kick-backs for the mother, wouldn't it be better to finish the whole thing quickly with an early abortion? Then the girl's life can return to normal with a minimum of bother. And anyway, add women's lib, isn't a girl to have control of her own body and be able to say what happens to it?

To me this issue is not primarily a Christian one. As the Bible says nothing directly I find myself listening to what all the experts, Christian and non-Christian say. I find they're split right down the middle. Doctors, psychiatrists, sociologists and lawyers, all of them disagree among themselves. That makes it tough for an ordinary bloke like me. What am I to think?

First of all it's pretty clear that we have to find out a lot more about the after effects of abortion. Until recently a lot of people said that providing the abortion was expertly done there needn't be any. We know now that this is not true. Reports say that 10% of abortions lead to physical complications and that up to 5% may make it difficult for those girls to have children in future.

However, it is not the physical problems that matter most. Some studies suggest that 25% of girls who have abortions have psychological kick-backs more serious than just feeling a bit guilty. But other studies suggest the percentage is much lower. At the moment the answer is not clear. All I know is that just in my few contacts, I've come across more than one girl who has cracked up on the very day when the baby she didn't have would have been due.

It begins to look as though, once a girl gets pregnant, she just can't get back to square one, whatever she does. Pregnancy is so basic a part of a woman's experience of life that it leaves its psychological mark, even if it is terminated quite early.

So get it straight that abortion is as much a psychological problem as a physical one. That's another argument against amateur operators. They only do half the job, the physical part. They can't give the psychological care at the time or afterwards, and the way they have to work slickly and impersonally tends to lead to psychological problems for the girl. If it is to be an abortion, then be sure you get the proper psychological care you may need.

A pregnant single girl has to find the best way out of her situation, but no way is free of snags. The solution that seems easiest in the moment of strife may not be best in the long run, but that's not easy to see when you're actually in the jam. This is where a girl needs professional advice and it's why I don't think I favour abortion on demand. Left to herself the girl may not make the best choice. A sympathetic doctor is more likely to weigh up the emotional problems of going through the pregnancy against the psychological and other risks of an abortion. I'm just glad I'm not the poor doctor!

11

Four problem areas

You'll know from the newspapers that kinky sex is a big field, far too big for one little chapter in a small book. Anyway you don't straighten out somebody with a sex abnormality through a book. The purpose of this chapter is more to clue-up those who have a 'normal' outlook, about some of the 'abnormal' sex you may come up against.

Homosexuality

The term refers to sexual relations between two people of the same sex, as opposed to normal heterosexual relations. 'Homos' and 'heteros' are Greek words meaning 'same' and 'different'. When the two people are women, the term 'lesbianism' is commonly used to describe the relationship. Homosexual relations take many forms. The two commonest are mutual masturbation, in which the couple stimulate each others' sex organs to orgasm and, secondly, the insertion of the penis in the anal opening of the other person, called sodomy or buggery. Many slang terms are used to describe homosexuals and their actions. The homosexual circle has tended to adopt the label 'gay' from among the various nicknames.

Homosexual practices are firmly condemned in the

few Bible references to them,[1] but the Bible says nothing at all about the homosexual *condition*. That's quite different from the typical modern approach. Psychologists today try to find out what causes the homosexual practices and, quite rightly, they are more concerned about treating that underlying condition than fussing about the actions themselves. That tends to give people the idea that homosexuals can't help themselves, so let them get on with it. In a few cases it appears true that little can be done to change a person's outlook, but not too many. Let's look at the three main types of homosexual and you'll see what I mean.

(a) *The physiological homosexual*
There is a small group of people whose bodies are in fact sexually abnormal; they are called hermaphrodites. That term describes a range of conditions where a person has some or all of the sex organs of one sex, but the hormonal balance and emotions tend to be like the other sex. It is from this group that the sex-change stories come. Their problem is a medical one and only suitably qualified doctors can help them. Fortunately they are a very small minority.

(b) *The psychological homosexual*
The next group consists of people who are genuinely attracted to members of their own, rather than the opposite, sex for emotional and psychological reasons. It is a much larger group than the first, though still only a small proportion of society. Nobody really has accurate figures because it is so difficult to

[1] Leviticus 18.22, 20.13; Romans 1.27; 1 Corinthians 6.9–10; 1 Timothy 1.9, 10.

distinguish between them and the third category, even if you can identify homosexuals, which is hard enough.

A typical psychological explanation of this kind of homosexual condition goes something like this. Children go through a phase of relating mainly to their own sex and ignoring the opposite sex. This usually happens in upper primary school. If a teenage boy lacks an effective father, he may find it hard to relate to women other than his mother. He gets hung up in his emotional development and continues to relate better to other men than to women. Physical maturity naturally brings a sexual dimension to such relationships. If you look at it this way, the resultant homosexuality is a form of immaturity.

The condition can be treated by psychiatrists, but psychiatrists can only get good results with those who really want help. A lot of homosexuals seem to be pretty half-hearted in the way they look for help. Lack of confidence in the sexual side of life affects the rest of their make-up and they tend to be or become what the psychologists call 'inadequate personalities' in general. So they 'drop out' by settling with others of their own kind. Their situation has its problems, but it's more comfortable than trying to fight against the tide. So they become hard to help.

The problem comes through very clearly in *The Returns of Love*,[1] one of the best Christian books about homosexuality. Any Christian who wants to understand the feelings of a homosexual should read this book. It brings out the sadness, almost the hopelessness, of the homosexual's position, but one also finds

[1] *The Returns of Love* by Alex Davidson (Inter Varsity Press).

oneself admiring the author for his clearcut stand as a Christian. Just because he's more interested in his own sex, he has no more right to be promiscuous than the heterosexual has. He has the same responsibility to exercise sexual self-control, with the added problem that marriage offers him no long-term prospect of sexual satisfaction. For him it will have to be sublimation of his sexual drive throughout life.

In case you are worried by what you have just read, because you feel you recognize some of these tendencies in yourself, let me add two things. First, read the next section. Then, if you are still worried, go and get advice from someone whom you trust. A school counsellor, social worker, doctor or clergyman may be good people to try, or you may prefer to go to some adult friend you like and respect.

(c) *Circumstantial homosexuals*

Most of us are a strange mixture of feelings and emotions. That applies to sex, too. A lot of people have some capacity for homosexual attraction, but living a normal life they never have any need or chance to give expression to it. However, if all contact with the opposite sex is denied, as in prisons, prisoner-of-war camps, monasteries and old-style boarding schools, then people who are basically quite normal sexually may get drawn into homosexual relations. They have become homosexual by circumstances.

The big argument is whether they are likely to stay that way afterwards. It probably varies with different individuals. Many, no doubt, go back to their normal sexual role but some of those who have adopted the 'opposite sex' role in the homosexual situation, and who found it congenial, may well stay partly or wholly that way. If they practise sex relations with either sex they are called 'bisexual'.

You don't have to do time to come up against homosexuality, especially if you spend some of your life in boarding school or the armed services. You are quite likely to come up against homosexual people in ordinary life, and I can only give you one kind of advice. Keep clear of what they are doing. It may not do you much harm, but there is a chance that it might and it certainly can't do you any good. It can only make it harder for you to relate normally to the opposite sex.

So how do you react to homosexual people? That is a different question. Jesus loves everybody, even those who make a complete mess of sex in their lives. Most of us Christians don't copy him too well. We disapprove of homosexuality, so we make it tough for homosexuals when they need our care and understanding more than most. Remember that their homosexual feelings may be unfortunate but the feelings themselves aren't wrong. Many homosexuals control their feelings better than many heterosexuals do. And if they don't? Is the practising homosexual any worse than the person who sleeps around with the opposite sex? Both are people who need understanding and love.

Prostitution

The 'oldest profession', as it is sometimes called, involves a woman having sexual intercourse with a man for money. Occasionally it happens the other way around, too, but that's uncommon. A house where a group of prostitutes operate is called a 'brothel'. Prostitution is a complex subject, but there are three things about it that might matter for those likely to be reading this book.

First, you will inevitably come across reports in the press and in other places and you need to know what to make of those reports. It's commonly suggested that lonely men in mostly male set-ups ought to be provided with supervised brothels. The supporters of legalized or controlled prostitution say that you can at least keep disease in check, because you can give the prostitutes regular medical check-ups. Where prostitution is illegal, you drive it underground and then you've no idea at all where to find the girls that need checking on.

This kind of argument from a purely social standpoint can be made to sound pretty convincing. Another one is that making prostitution illegal plays into the hands of the standover men who tend to be involved in the business. There is probably some truth in this argument, though legislation can't stamp out the main blackmail element. There are too many customers who want to keep their visit to a prostitute quiet from somebody. In this and other ways prostitution gets tied in with the shady side of society. It's hard to say how the social arguments balance out.

However, the social view is only one way of looking at the problem. I feel the personal angle is much more important. After all, prostitutes are people and so are the men involved with them. Sex is basically about the relationships between people. When you look at prostitution from this angle, there's hardly a good thing to be said for it. The money – or big present or other favour, it's all the same – kills any emotional element stone dead. It makes sex about as low as it can get. The woman's just doing a job; the man's just paying for sexual relief.

The man is only involved casually and perhaps occasionally and he may not be affected much as a person, but for the prostitute who's involved all the time it's quite different. A fair summary is that it destroys her ability to respond emotionally as a normal woman should; it robs her of most of the satisfactions which a woman expects to find in life and leaves her with nothing, often not even much money.

Now it may not always look or be as crude as that. What about the girl who latches on to a rich boy and quite enjoys the sex part of the deal? Why shouldn't she accept the mink coat he offers her? What's the difference between that and the wife who accepts the big bunch of flowers her husband brings home? The answer is in the motives of each party in the couple concerned. We might not be able to read other people's motives but if we're honest we can usually read our own motives clearly enough.

Poverty, or just being broke, pushes some girls into prostitution. It looks an easy way to earn some desperately needed cash.

It is important to realize just where you can end up if you offer a guy sex for what he'll give you in cash or kind. In some circumstances a girl may well be tempted to earn a fast buck on the side. Quite a few professional prostitutes start this way. The girl may be pregnant and want money for an abortion. She sees a quick way of making it and, after all, she can't get any more pregnant, and that's how she starts in the oldest profession. Any girl thinking in that direction wants to take a long, hard look at how most 'pros' are exploited and where they end up. If you do that, you won't take the chance.

There's not much in going with a prostitute for the guy either. For a start it's likely to be pretty poor quality sex. Secondly, there's bound to be an above-average risk of infection. But, far more important, think what you're doing to the pair of you. O.K., if it's not 'you' she'll hire herself to someone else. But do you want to be the one who helps to wreck another human being? If you're too selfish to care about her, then think of yourself and how your appreciation of sex is lowered.

As a parting shot for the Christian, I might remind you of that passage in 1 Corinthians 6.12–20 mentioned in chapter six. If you read that, there's nothing else that needs to be said.

Rape

Rape occurs when a man compels a woman to have sexual intercourse with him against her will, either by physical force or by other threats. It is one of the most serious crimes in the statute book and rightly so, because being raped can deprive a girl of the capacity for sexual pleasure for the rest of her life. Yet sometimes the girl asks for trouble by the way she behaves and the places she goes to.

A study is now being done on rape cases in Australia in recent years. A preliminary report suggests that motor vehicles and alcohol are commonly associated with them. The first is obvious enough. The easiest way to get a girl to yourself is to take her off to a lonely spot in a car. The alcohol connection is more complicated. Alcohol, in fact, lowers rather than raises sexual desire. But it also lowers inhibitions, self-control and discrimination, the last being possibly the vital factor.

In many rapes it seems that the girl doesn't object to the attentions of the guy at first. She may actually egg him on, or just not knock him back hard enough. She may quite enjoy the necking session. Often she has the reputation of being easy to get, because of the way she dresses, talks or acts, or because she's had sex with the guy (or one of the guys) before. It's only when the passion gets a bit hot that she gets scared and objects. By then it's often too late.

The guy has to read her mind. Is she really objecting, or just playing hard to get? Sometimes it's hard to tell. His discrimination, that is his ability to tell one thing from another, has been affected by alcohol and lets him down. So he pushes on regardless, perhaps really believing that the girl wants him to and there you are – he's on a rape charge.

So, you may decide, mother's advice about not getting into cars with strange guys, especially those who've been drinking, was right on target. So it is, nearly – but not quite. Another, more surprising, finding of this Australian research into rape is that the majority of the girls knew the men who raped them before the assault. So it isn't just *strange* men, but men known to you that you have to watch, girls. Whether you know the guy or not may be less important than the circumstances you get yourself into, the way you behave from the start and the kind of girl you're known (or thought) to be. The decent girl, who's sensible about where she goes alone, is very unlikely to be raped.

Incest

Incest is the name for sexual relations between close relatives, most commonly between a man and his daughter, or between brother and sister. It is a very serious offence against the law, but, in spite of that, it happens quite often and most cases go unreported. The reason is simply that few girls want to get their fathers or brothers into the big trouble which would come from blowing the gaff. So they let it go on and often suffer for the rest of their lives as a result. I am not exaggerating. Being seduced by her father is almost sure to make sex a disgusting thing to a girl. The psychological damage will make it difficult to enjoy sexual relations later in life, affecting her whole prospect of a relaxed and happy marriage.

So what should you do if you come up against this problem either in your life or in trying to help one of your friends? There are two parts to the answer. Firstly, you need help to stop the incest going on and your best bet for that is probably a clergyman or your doctor. If you don't feel either will do for you, choose the adult you feel you can trust best. Tell them in complete secrecy what is going on, and work out with them what to do. Once that part of the problem is solved, the next step is to get some psychological help to try to undo any damage which has been done. The sooner you do that, the easier it will be in the long run. Again, the friend you have chosen will be able to help you find the best person for this kind of help.

12

Sex (God's way) is happiness

All you have read, and more, Tony got from Dave, his club leader, over about six months. He'd been surprised at first how often Dave found an answer for a today's problem from the Bible. Solid answers too, not the muddled waffle which didn't add up, that you got from the kids who had no clear standards to live by. Then, one day, an off-the-cuff argument with some of the guys about Bob and Judy's situation had brought them all knocking on Dave's door. Next thing the whole group was having a big discussion on it instead of the usual Sunday afternoon Bible study groups. They ended with so many unanswered questions that they had to have another discussion a month later.

Now the group was just finishing a third long discussion in Dave and Carol's lounge-room. Tony felt good. Mostly it was because of Jan, but today it was Judy too. It was really good to see her there, back for the first time after having the baby. Boy, had they all made her welcome, too! Jan had seen to that. Did Judy realize how much she owed to Jan? Tony wondered. When Judy stopped coming around the club, because her being pregnant was getting so obvious, it was Jan who suggested they take their

Sunday Bible study to Judy's place.

They weren't too welcome at first.

'I don't want the Bible study here,' Judy said bluntly.

'Why not?' asked Jan.

'Because I don't, that's all. Just leave me alone.'

'Don't you want to be in the group any more?'

'It's nothing to do with what I want. I can't, can I?'

'Well, of course you don't want to come around the club for a while,' said Jan, 'but you're still part of the group.'

They'd argued like that for ages. In the end it was Judy's mother who'd told her to stop being silly and be thankful she had such good friends.

At first the guys, especially, found it a bit embarrassing, but after a few weeks no one thought a thing about Judy being pregnant. Then came that memorable afternoon. No one could remember afterwards how it started, but there they all were, discussing openly with Judy what she should do – keep the baby or have it adopted. Judy's mother just about dropped the afternoon tea tray when she heard what was going on; but everyone was so in it that they just went on arguing as though she hadn't come in.

They got so involved together that it seemed quite natural when, a few weeks later, Judy told the group what she'd decided. She wasn't keeping the baby, she announced firmly, because she thought it would have the best chance in a family that badly wanted it. No one knew what to say; it was the most embarrassing moment since they'd been going to Judy's. They got by somehow, but it was a long, powerful, silence.

All the same, it made no difference next Sunday,

which was the last as it happened, because Judy went to hospital the next week. Now here she was, back with them – really one of them, too, more so than before. Judy had really come out on top, Tony decided.

Pity he couldn't say the same about Bob. He'd tried to get Bob in on the first of the discussions on sex, but he wouldn't be in it. 'D'you expect me to come so they can take potshots at me over Judy?' was all he'd said. Then he really let Tony have it for the lousy friend he'd been to him. That had hurt. No, Bob didn't seem to want to learn from what had happened and none of them had seen him for weeks. The talk was he had a new girl over the other side of town and spent most of his time there these days.

Tony's thoughts shifted to Jan. She was looking his way and their eyes met. She was happy about Judy, he could see. 'The first time' – he got a shock as he realized – 'the first time I've known exactly what she's thinking, without her saying a word.' Yes, Jan and he were getting quite close.

That had come from his talks with Dave, too. Not that Dave had talked him into anything. The other way, if anything. But one night Dave and he had been talking about the man's part and the girl's part in a friendship. Tony had come a long way since that first half-hearted try at dating Jan. He'd only been a real Christian a few months, but getting life sorted out had somehow helped him grow up. He knew what he wanted this time. He wasn't jumping at any girl. He'd watched Jan for a while and everything he saw made him want to know her better. So this time he wasn't taking 'no' for an answer.

Jan was stunned at Tony's strong line. Six months ago she'd been telling a youngster to drop dead, though actually she was younger than him. This time Tony was different. As Jan listened to his invitation, Jan now saw a guy she really liked and wanted to go out with. The way she accepted made Tony feel a million dollars. No taking him for granted and no giggling the way most girls do, getting a guy all embarrassed. She just looked him straight in the eye and said quietly, 'Thanks, Tony, I'd really like that.'

The film wasn't much, but over coffee afterwards they'd talked. It wasn't specially personal but Tony had never talked like that with a girl before. They seemed to have lots to talk about, without even trying. Tony asked her again. She didn't refuse, but she couldn't see when. Study all week, club on Friday, church on Sunday. It only left Saturday, when there wasn't a club committee or a family do.

Tony had to wait five weeks for Jan's next free Saturday. He wanted to take her to a film but they were all X certificates. Finally Jan said, 'Why not just come round to my place?' Tony was scared stiff. He hadn't reckoned on meeting Jan's folks yet awhile. He would have got out of it if he could, but he couldn't really say no and, actually, it was good. They hadn't done anything much, but somehow, after seeing Jan at home, he just knew her tons better. Looking back, that night was a real turning point. That was three weeks ago and they still hadn't made the cinema, but with luck they would next Saturday.

They did. The film was a riot, which helped. Coming back at the interval with ice creams, he noticed the couple across the aisle still wrapped around each other. He was glad they were his side. He and Jan lounged in their seats, sucked their ice creams and just talked – about Jan's family, about Judy, about the club and the special discussions.

'They've really sorted me out,' Tony said. 'I wish other kids could get sex straight like that.'

'You mean the couple over there?' Jan teased.

'Didn't know you could see. I wasn't thinking of them, but of Bob and some of the other guys around.'

'Yes, of course.'

'Still, talking of next door . . .' he paused.

'What, Tony?'

'Oh – just that I find I . . . I . . . well, I just wouldn't want to try the heavy stuff.'

'You'd better not.'

'O.K., I know I wouldn't get far, but that's not what I meant. I wasn't thinking of your angle, but of how I feel, inside. I just don't want to.'

Jan said nothing.

'It's just great to sit and talk and get to know you.'

She smiled.

'Somehow sex doesn't come into it.'

'Thanks!' she said sharply, 'That really makes a girl feel great!'

'Oh, cut it out! I didn't mean it like that.' Tony was embarrassed. Things Dave had said came at him from all sides.

'If sex doesn't come into it . . .' Jan went on, but Tony stopped her.

'Of course it does, Jan, in a way, but . . . but . . .' He couldn't find the words he wanted.

'Not that way,' Jan prompted, nodding across the aisle.

'That's it.' Tony sank back and relaxed. She did understand after all. She'd had him on a string, beautifully, the little so-and-so. Boy, he liked her style. There was silence for a while. He was just working around to what he wanted to say when the film came on again. So it had to wait.

As the film ended and everybody got up, Tony did nothing to move.

'No hurry,' he said.

'No.'

'Jan, there's something important.'

'Yes?'

'I was working around to it at the interval, but you . . .'

'I teased you. Sorry, Tony, I shouldn't have, but you really laid yourself open to kidding. I just couldn't stop myself.'

'No, that's O.K. Jan, I asked for it. But what I was trying to say was that I'm serious. I haven't just wanted the fun of a night out.'

'I know. I wouldn't have come otherwise, if I hadn't been serious, too.'

'I realized that, because you wouldn't be in it before. But what I tried to say at the interval when I got all fouled up . . .'

'When I fouled you up!'

'. . . was that when it's serious and you're Christians, O.K., I shouldn't have said sex isn't there, but it's way down below somewhere.'

'Where it ought to be, Tony.'

'O.K., yes, that's right, but it's good that way.'

'You make me really happy, Tony.' The look she gave him stopped him talking.

He grabbed her arm and pushed past the manager closing the cinema doors. A hundred yards down the road he found words.

'Jan, I've been thinking all night of what Dave said last Sunday. "Sex – God's way – is happiness!" '

'He sure was right, wasn't he, Tony?'

'Just so right, and that's just how we've got to keep it.'

Other books you could read

The Stork is Dead   C. W. Shedd   (*Word Books*)
A really readable book for teenagers, containing practical information and advice.

Love is a Feeling to be Learned   Walter Trobisch(*IVP*)

I Loved a Girl   Walter Trobisch   (*Lutterworth*)

I Married You   Walter Trobisch   (*IVP*)
Writing from the African scene, Walter Trobisch manages to give a picture of what real love is all about anywhere in the world.

A Love Story   Tim Stafford   (*Lakeland*)
Based on replies to letters on sex received at 'Campus Life' magazine, this book tackles a wide range of problems, including masturbation, shyness, and many more.

Boy/Girl Relationships   Simon Matthews   (*Good News Crusade*)
A clear-sighted biblical discussion. Short and meaty.

Understanding the Christian and Sex   M. O. Vincent (*Scripture Union*)
The best general book for adults, young and old, that I know. 'Christian Graduate' called it 'the most wise general work on sex we've seen for a long time'.

Christianity and Sexual Liberation   Peter Cousins
(Paternoster)

A good little book for the younger teenagers, to start you on the right lines about marriage, adultery, homosexuality and the rest.

What about Abortion?   R. F. R. Gardiner *(Paternoster)*

A simple summary, by one of the top Christian authorities on the subject, of the issues raised by this difficult topic. He doesn't try to give slick answers, either!

The Returns of Love   Alex Davidson   *(IVP)*

I don't know of a simple little book on this subject. This sad book describes what it feels like to be a Christian and have strong homosexual drives.

If you have specific medical or biological queries or problems, don't be afraid to discuss them with your doctor, who normally will treat such queries completely confidentially if you wish. He or she will be able to direct you to suitable books or pamphlets if the books mentioned above don't deal with what you want to read about.